The Soul of the City

Mapping the Spiritual Geography of Eleven Canadian Cities

Leonard Hjalmarson

Endorsements

As more urban practitioners explore the contributions of spiritual geography to understanding and engaging theologically with their contexts, this collection of essays from Canadian cities helpfully shows how this can be applied and demonstrates its potential.

Stuart Murray-Williams
National Director
Urban Expression UK

Canadian cities are fascinating to study. They are even better as places where one lives. This anthology is a masterful contribution from practitioners who live in our city/regions and choose to articulate a missional theology from their lived experiences. This is an invaluable contribution to the literature.

Glenn Smith, Missiologist
Executive Director of Christian Direction (Montréal)
Academic Dean of Institut de théologie pour la Francophonie of Université Laval

The Soul of the City
Mapping the Spiritual Geography of Eleven Canadian Cities

Copyright © 2018 Leonard Hjalmarson

All rights reserved. Except for brief quotations in critical publications or reviews, no part of this book may be reproduced in any manner without prior written permission from the publisher. Write: Permissions, Urban Loft Publishers, P.O. Box 6
Skyforest, CA, 92385.

Urban Loft Publishers
P.O. Box 6
Skyforest, CA 92385
www.urbanloftpublishers.com

Senior Editors: Stephen Burris & Kendi Howells Douglas
Copy Editor: Christian Arnold
Graphics: Morgan Simms, Elisabeth Arnold
Image Art Credit: Renée De Gagné

Scripture quotations are from the New Revised Standard Version Bible, copyright © 1989 National Council of the Churches of Christ in the United States of America. Used by permission. All rights reserved.

ISBN-13: 978-0-9989177-6-4

Made in the U.S

Series Preface

Urban Mission in the 21st Century is a series of monographs that addresses key issues facing those involved in urban ministry whether it be in the slums, squatter communities, *favelas*, or in immigrant neighborhoods. It is our goal to bring fresh ideas, a theological basis, and best practices in urban mission as we reflect on our changing urban world. The contributors to this series bring a wide-range of ideas, experiences, education, international perspectives, and insight into the study of the growing field of urban ministry. These contributions fall into four very general areas: 1--the biblical and theological basis for urban ministry; 2--best practices currently in use and anticipated in the future by urban scholar/activists who are living working and studying in the context of cities; 3--personal experiences and observations based on urban ministry as it is currently being practiced; and 4--a forward view toward where we are headed in the decades ahead in the expanding and developing field of urban mission. This series is intended for educators, graduate students, theologians, pastors, and serious students of urban ministry.

More than anything, these contributions are creative attempts to help Christians strategically and creatively think about how we can better reach our world that is now more urban than rural. We do not see theology and practice as separate and distinct. Rather, we see sound practice growing out of a healthy vibrant theology that seeks to understand God's world as it truly is as we move further into the twenty-first century. Contributors interact with the best scholarly literature available at the time of writing while making application to specific contexts in which they live and work.

Each book in the series is intended to be a thought-provoking work that represents the author's experience and perspective on urban ministry in a particular context. The editors have chosen those who bring this rich diversity of perspectives to this series. It is our hope and prayer that each book in this series will challenge, enrich, provoke, and cause the reader to dig deeper into subjects that bring the reader to a deeper understanding of our urban world and the ministry the church is called to perform in that new world.

Dr. Kendi Howells Douglas and Stephen Burris,
Urban Mission in the 21st Century Series Co-Editors

Table of Contents

Series Preface...4

Table of Contents..6

Foreword...7

Introduction..13

Chapter 1- Victoria..25

Chapter 2- Vancouver, BC...45

Chapter 3- Kelowna, BC...65

Chapter 4- Edmonton, Alberta..85

Chapter 5- Calgary, Alberta..109

Chapter 6- Regina, Saskatchewan..................................133

Chapter 7- Winnipeg, Manitoba.....................................149

Chapter 8- Toronto, Ontario...167

Chapter 9- Ottawa, Ontario..191

Chapter 10- Montreal, Quebec......................................207

Chapter 11- Halifax, Nova Scotia..................................227

FOREWORD
Donald Goertz

This particular book holds great significance to us as the Church in Canada. Although it neither presents great answers, nor provides immediate solutions to the problems which nag at us, it is rich in insights. This book engages us in a critical conversation, a conversation that captures our attention with the intriguing question, "What is the soul of the city?" Very few of us would have considered asking this question prior to seeing the title of this book. Yet it is a question that needs to move increasingly into the forefront of our reflection.

In order to begin to think about the significance of the soul of a city, we must first comprehend that we currently reside in a predominantly urban nation. At a personal level, this is a live issue for me. I *live* in a community which is now the largest town in Canada. It has a population of well over 200,000. Yet, it insists that it is not a city, but rather a town. Why? Because claiming cityhood communicates something about the soul of the community which most residents perceive as negative–less friendly.

Moreover, I lead a program concentration at Tyndale Seminary entitled Church in the City. When prospective students hear about this, even though the majority live in Toronto and its surrounding cities, most will insist that these courses do not apply to them because they do not live in the city, but in a suburb. And there is our tension. Many of us see the city as negative–a place to be avoided if one can afford it. It is this ambiguity that allows me to approach this book with such optimism.

One of the fastest growing fields in Canada right now is that of urban studies. The rapidly changing landscape of our nation has made this not only an interesting field of research, but an essential one, demanding deeper engagement and understanding. Once described as a nation defined by its land, Canada self-identified as a place of wide spaces, wilderness and farms. No one captured this more evocatively than the group of painters, the Group of Seven. They gave us images of our nation which tapped into a deep experience of nature.

The same was true for generations of writers. Understanding Canada required traversing vast distances on often poor roads. The vastness and power of the land was inescapable. The early stories that shaped us, Susanna Moody's 1852 book *Roughing It in the Bush,* or George Munro Grant's 1873 vision of nation, *Ocean to Ocean,* spoke of the beauty, wonder and potential of the land. Modern story tellers, such as Farley Mowat, continued the tradition, providing us with libraries of stories touching every region of the nation, and deeply rooted in the land. Yet even a century ago, something else simmered below the surface.

Both the Wilfred Laurier and Clifford Sifton eras at the end of the 19th and early 20th century launched a wave of immigration on an unimagined scale. City missionaries like J. S. Woodsworth in his 1908 work, *The Strangers Within Our Gates,* began to describe a new, emerging immigrant reality which was unsettling, but became the next challenge for the Church and the nation. While these changes abated and lost their urgency with the war in 1914, they have emerged again with a vengeance since the 1960s, as wave after wave of immigrants from all corners of the world arrived to remake the nation and especially the city. Immigrants have dramatically stretched and reshaped our cities. Our urban centres are now cosmopolitan, pluralistic, multi-cultural communities with identities not yet set. Our cities, and with them our nation, are in seemingly constant transition.

While there is no doubt that the vast expanse of land still defines our nation, it no longer anchors the experience of the current generation of Canadians. Today the land is something one flies over as we move from one city to another. Like the vision of New York in Michel de Certeau's, *The Practice of Everyday Life,* we view the world from high above while traveling between cities, detached, while simultaneously watching a movie. When we do engage the wilderness, it is only to exploit resources or to enjoy recreational activity. Whether it is the work camps or the resorts or the experience of nature as encountered by a Lawren Harris, Emily Carr or Tom Thomson, we only enter into the land supplied with the latest amenities and equipment. Our goal is to pursue the experience while eliminating the discomfort. We have become de Certeau's voyeurs. Simultaneously, as Woodsworth observed, we are a nation comprised of strangers, arriving from every corner of the world.

This new urban reality began a re-imagining of the city. It began in places like Toronto and Vancouver where industrialization and immigration were the most dramatic. What did it mean to be a city; a neighbourhood? For most of us, we imagined a city as little more than a really large town. Urban was a word used to describe the small central core and for most, this meant height. But soon alternative voices emerged, Jane Jacobs being the most significant, giving us new language, an urban poetics, an imagination with which to query our experience in these rapid new environments. Today Canada is one of the leading centres for urban studies. It is a field of research which is growing by necessity. The urban footprint[1] of our census metropolitan areas includes almost everyone in the nation. We are a profoundly urban nation.

As a church we have lagged far behind in our understanding of the city. Very few congregations see themselves as communities wrestling with what it means to be salt and light in the urban landscape. We have not been intentional around thinking about the places where we are located and how we might engage them. In Sheldrake's book, *Spaces for the Sacred*, he reminds us that we have missed the particularities and tend to regard place as merely a container where one receptacle is just as good as another. The city is the container in which we live and work, and our church buildings are not locations, but merely set-pieces on the stage, positioned to facilitate maximum ease of access from all points in the region. That sets up the problem we have for renewed engagement, in a world where virtuality and reality are intertwined.

As you work your way through this book, you will see a wide range of approaches and definitions to the question of the soul of the city. To his credit, Hjalmarson did not provide definitions for the authors. The guidelines were

---

[1] An urban footprint refers to the social, economic and cultural impact of the city which stretches far beyond its geographic boundaries. Recently social media has dramatically expanded this urban footprint. For a fuller discussion of this see Andrew Davey's book *Urban Christianity and the Global Order, Theological Resources for an Urban Future* (London: SPCK, 2001).

designed to stimulate creativity and allow for each city to be approached in its own unique way. You will quickly notice this.

And this book adds a unique feature. It goes back to the beginning. Central to the questions which Hjalmarson raises for the authors to engage is the place of First Nations in the city. This is a question of how we understand our narrative. Is it a longer narrative, one in which First Nations roots play a larger role? Or, does the story of the city begin with the arrival of the settlers? Again, this is a key *soul* question, but one which few churches are addressing. We are churches of settlers. One gift this book offers is its challenge to place this question of First Nations/ Settlers in the forefront of our reading of the city. As you engage the authors you will feel their wrestling with how best to engage this aspect of our soul.

Each author approached their city differently. They were looking for language and categories to make sense of something they see as important. We enter into their wrestling with these tensions. Simple decisions have a profound effect on how the story is told. Do they approach the question from the perspective of the community in which they live and work or from that of the larger whole in which the community is located? How do neighborhoods and cities fit together and define and shape each other? Some authors work from the perspective of the whole and try to approach the question from that lens. Others consider the city from their own location. This has generated a wide variety to the work.

As you read, be attentive to the perspective and location of each author and how it shapes their chapter. Watch for the ways in which ministry context provides language and categories for reflection. Let them challenge you with the tension between the history of the city/neighbourhood and its current context. Ask questions around difference and similarity. In these various approaches we see the kaleidoscope of the question and are broadened in our own understanding.

Above all, focus on the common thread that artists weave in the tapestry of community renewal. Note how frequently artists–from guerrilla graffiti artists to structured artist groups, to artists who lead us to realms of creativity and beauty in worship–play a central role in helping a community to find hope, to reimagine a future and to find new ways forward in times of transition. Artists always seem to be those who lead us.

For me, this book will have fulfilled a vital role for us as the Canadian church if we as readers allow each chapter to generate a new conversation with us, one that pushes us to understand the soul of our own city. But don't get caught in the moment. Allow yourself space to ask the longer-view questions. The Canadian city is still an undefined entity, constantly evolving, with the kind of fluidity Bauman notes as a quality of late Modernity. Don't seek for certainty or closure. Rather, let this be an entry point for you to delve into the unfolding story of your city or neighbourhood.

Donald Goertz

Associate Professor of Church History
Director, Church in the City
Tyndale University College and Seminary

Hjalmarson

INTRODUCTION

Len Hjalmarson

It's survival in the city
When you live from day to day
City streets don't have much pity
When you're down, that's where you'll stay.

(The Eagles, 2003)

The classic Eagles song tells one side of the story. William Cronon notes that for many of us cities have "represented all that [is] most unnatural about human life... a cancer on an otherwise beautiful landscape" (Cronon, 1992, p. 17). This dualistic view has the negative effect of limiting creative and redemptive engagement in our urban places. We must move beyond the duality of country equals good, and urban equals bad. A more nuanced engagement is needed. *Soul of the City* is a move in this direction.

Show me your city and I will show you what it is you long for. (Ward, 2003. p. 467)

Let's begin with a few foundational questions for our study. First, "What is a city? Is a city different than a town or a hamlet? Is a city defined by population, geography, or function, or some combination of these?" In his book *The City Shaped*, Spiro Kostoff (1991) offers two popular definitions for the city, both dating back to 1938. In *Nature's Metropolis* Cronon (1992) writes, "For L. Wirth, a city is a 'restively large, dense, and permanent settlement of socially heterogeneous individuals.' For Mumford, a city is a 'point of maximum concentration for the power and culture of a community'" (p. 26). More recently, Tim Keller (2009) defined a city as a walkable, shared, mixed-use, diverse area; a place of commerce, residence, culture and politics. This is what we call a *functional* definition.

Broadly speaking there are three models of city, organized by function. Architect Kevin Lynch (1960) delineates these as *cosmic, practical, and organic*. The *cosmic* city is designed to reflect the core of a belief system. Ancient Chinese capitals were laid out in perfect squares, with their twelve gates representing the months of the year. The *practical* city is imagined after a machine, and grows as new parts are added and old parts altered. New York is a practical city.[2] The third type is the *organic* city. In this model functions are arranged organically, with cohesion, access and function acting together. Streets may meander, and neighbourhoods and boroughs are joined together in the greater labyrinth. London, England is a good example of an organic city, as are Portland, Oregon and Vancouver, BC.[3]

Second, "Why concern ourselves with the city?" More than 80% of Canadians now live in cities, and this proportion will increase. The city, not the country, is the place where most people will exercise their "skilled mastery"[4] in this century. This moves our skilled-mastery beyond farming and craftsmanship to shaping the urban landscape. This

---

[2] Sean Benesh prefers an alternative approach to functionality, classifyng cities by the transportation technologies around which they organize: walking cities, transit cities and automobile cities. *The Multi-Nucleated Church* (Portland: Urban Loft Publishers, 2011), 18-19.

[3] All three of these are also "multi-nucleated," or "polycentric," where dispersal and densification play off one another.

[4] A translation of the Hebrew word *radah* in Genesis 1.

new emphasis in skilled mastery translates into place-making[5] in the city. Jacques Ellul (1970) writes,

> The city dweller becomes someone else because of the city. And the city can become something else because of God's presence and the results in the life of a man [sic] who has met God. And so a complex cacophony raises its blaring voice, and only God can see and make harmony of it. (p. 44)

Not only do we shape the city, but the city will shape us. Will our environment make us more human, or less? Will our urban places help us to thrive, and offer us a context for *shalom*, encouraging practices that make space for the Kingdom? Even in the city, place-making is determined by a master-story.[6]

This leads to our third question: "Why should Christians focus on the city?" I'm interested in spiritual formation, and cities are enormous factories for culture. Culture in turn forms us into certain kinds of people, and as followers of the Way character matters to us. Still more, cities generate *cruciality*: they are crucibles for change more than any other environment. We must pay more attention to the city. *Project for Public Spaces* (2012) remarks, "As much as we prize creativity in cities today, the cultural centers that we've built to celebrate it rarely hit the mark. Culture is born out of human interaction; it therefore cannot exist without people around to enjoy, evaluate, remix, and participate in it."

The narratives which shape our cities are complex. The forces of global mapping privilege the universal in the name of profit. Graham

---

[5] Place-making is a sub-set of vocation is part of God's redemptive mission, and something we all do, often transparently. When we build, or paint a building, or plant trees, or decorate a coffee-shop, we are place-making. Caring for the environment is also an expression of place-making, and working for justice can be another.

[6] An over-arching narrative of the kind post-moderns are not fond of.

Ward (2005) writes that, "the major issues affecting a global city are increasingly less local, or even national – they are international. This is mainly because it is an international profile that the major cities of the world are competing for in order to attract investment." (p. 30) Thus the ability to make choices is often suspended, and transferred to multinational corporations where unelected leaders wield enormous power. Ramachandra (2006) identifies the "global village," in the sense of a mutually enriching exchange, as a myth.[7]

Graham Ward (2005) says that global cities are characterized by fear and anxiety. He writes that, "The global, post-secular city [London] is the home of the migrant soul. Citizens are caught between two public narratives: the potential violence of coexisting cultural differences, and the fear of the erasure of difference." (p. 39) He notes that both these narratives are totalitarian and depoliticizing (i.e. they do not lead to engagement). Ward (2005) argues that the alternative is a "practice of living that . . . negotiates difference without assimilation." (p. 39) Christians can offer the possibility of such an alternative.

Some say that tolerance is a Canadian virtue, and it is certainly an ideal to which liberal Canadian elites aspire. But tolerance is not a Christian ideal. Rather, our engagement is a politics of resistance rooted in a paradox. David Bentley Hart (2003) frames the paradox like this: "He is not the high who stands over against the low, but is the infinite act of existence that gives high and low a place" (p. 320). The essential practice is the Eucharist, which "creates space for the diversity of human voices to participate" (Sheldrake, 2001, p. 168). The Church is an anticipation of the eschatological humanity, with the Eucharist a

---

[7] Graham Ward argues that one answer to the depoliticization of politics is the practice of cultural hermeneutics: the analysis, examination and interpretation of cultural practices.

counter-narrative of globalization that builds the global Body of Christ in every *place*, with all its beautiful diversity.

But while we ought to live out a politics of resistance, that is not *all* we are. The church is not merely a resistance community. The Greek word *ekklesia* referenced a political body long before it was adopted by Christians. Our members occupy roles in the broader social landscape. The church thus has potential to work against the fragmentation of public and private, secular and sacred, rich and poor. Cities are often run by elites, but the church knows no such class structure, in fact it gives privilege to those *without* power. Thus our work in the city must also be prophetic. Let's look at this more closely.

Surveying the Spiritual Landscape

Geography is simply a visible form of theology. (Levenson, 1985, p. 116)

How do we get to know our cities? How do we identify the spirit of a place? What theological and social frameworks will contribute to our understanding? We have begun to sketch these above, but our theological frames are likely to be diverse, shaped by the contexts and traditions which shape us, and so the complexity of our analysis becomes uniquely dialogical and contextual.

We can reflect on a particular place in terms of what we may call the spiritual geography, extending the theological task into an exploration of how context impacts faith. We use the word "context" to describe a particular environment, including, but not limited to, the physical dimensions.[8] We include the historical, economic, social and cultural factors. Not only does context impact belief but also it provides a window (perhaps, an "imaginary") through which one may relate to

---

[8] I particularly value the work of two writers in this area: Clifford Geertz and his book *Local Knowledge* (Baker, 1983) and Clarence Sedmak, *Doing Local Theology* (Orbis Books, 2002)

God. Moreover, the rise of virtual and networked space complicates context. The authors of *Networked Theology* remind us that "geography becomes irrelevant as time-space barriers dissolve." (Campbell & Garner, 2016, p. 89)

When we extend the theological task to discern the spiritual geography of a place, we highlight the interweave of attitudes and environment, postures and politics, and the ways this interweave calls to the spirit or denigrates it. These things are commonly felt as intangibles, and are difficult to identify and articulate. Theology is a reflective task because it asks questions and makes statements it cannot understand. It's the nature of the craft. But our work helps us evaluate the human environment at levels that are more than merely phenomenological. It contributes to the richness of a spiritual vocabulary rooted in the rough and tumble of life, "sails and ships and ceiling wax" (Carroll, 1872). It is not just holy places which inspire us, but places which inspire us to *become holy*: they transform our human journey into a pilgrimage.

Linda Mercadante (2004) warns that discerning the spirit of a place could be reduced to a vague delineation of how a place is or is not conducive to human flourishing. She offers two safeguards to this tendency. First, the awareness that God is continually trying to reach us, to break through our defenses, and to offer divine grace. Second, as Calvin stressed, that God accommodates to our condition. "Our particularity creates the need for God to come to us in ways we can understand, and . . . God has the consummate ability to do this" (Mercadante, 2004, p. 62).

The most fundamental way God has met us is in the Incarnation. The Incarnation combined the human and divine, matter and spirit, and was preeminently a phenomenon of spatiality. Jesus was placed, a first century Jew meeting us in place and time. This may cue us to some important questions relative to our urban contexts. The physical space of our humanity is not just flesh and blood, but also steel and glass. Our bodies do not interact socially apart from physical places (though digital technology is a new kind of mediation). And in the nature of culture itself, our bodies participate in both a natural environment and cultural artifacts, so that the city is more than mere container, as place is more than space. *The city is us.*

There are a few other things to consider as you seek to understand your city. The city remains both graced and fallen. In his chapter in this book Rob Crosby-Shearer notes of Victoria that there are "shadows in paradise." Later in this book, Cory Seibel describes the darker "frontier" realities of Edmonton noting that these are "acute manifestations of phenomena that occur across the life of the city." Each of our cities needs this kind of nuanced mapping.

We can provide our cities with this assisted by the social critique of writers like Zizek, Baumann, and Chomsky. In Zizek, for example, the "both/and" experiences in our cities are called "irruptions." This enables him to move beyond the external psychological sign of an inner disturbance in his discussion of social symptoms (Zizek, 1989).

For Zizek, a symptom can work within a culture to expose an unfulfilled drive, the unspoken void around which that culture has been formed. "An image, an explosion of media activity surrounding an event, a popular movie, a flurry of publishing can expose something hidden and unspoken that drives a culture's meaning system" (Hesiak, 2007). What we see and hear on the surface may be compensations for what the culture itself lacks at its core. Exposing these kinds of Zizekian symptoms in our cities opens them up for change and transformation.

For Zizek, cultural symbolic orders exist to legitimize something; as such they are ideologies. These meaning systems mask an absence which no one wants to face. So every cultural system is prone to "irruptions of the Real" which reflect back to its participants what is hidden within the ongoing system of meaning. Thus the homeless populations amidst capitalist societies reveal the immanent logic of the politic of capitalism. This is poignantly clear in the chapter in this book penned by Spurgeon D. Root and Nick Helliwell, but features in a number of chapters in this book. Capitalist ideology may say that its goal is to rid humanity of all poverty, but Zizek would suggest that the homeless person reveals the true drive *behind* capitalism, the way it plays upon the fear of poverty and the fear that we all might become homeless if we don't work harder. Global capitalism is a force that impacts the soul of every large Western city, and its symptoms are available to any observer.

Finally, it's important to keep in mind that, while the city has always been amenable to new technologies, digital culture and new media are impacting our communities as never before. To the extent that these expressions of connectivity work against our neighbourly relationships they may act as a solvent to social capital. But the knife cuts both ways. To the extent that new technologies empower connection they may also lead to renewed civic engagement, a richer expression of the soul. The role of Twitter in the Occupy movement, as in the Arab Spring, are cases in point. Social geographers watch these developments with interest. Private space and public space are giving way to something like connected space, the in-between land of the other city that never sleeps: the Internet.[9] The soul of the city is also found in virtual space.

---

[9] The authors of *Networked Theology (2016)* describe "publicized privacy" and "constant contact" as part of the ambiguous nature of connective technologies. "Information ecology" now undergirds any real places we occupy.

Thirteen Practitioners

> "Walkers are 'practitioners of the city,' for the city is made to be walked. A city is a language, a repository of possibilities, and walking is the act of speaking that language, of selecting from those possibilities." (Solnit, 2000, p. 8)

We have gathered thirteen theological practitioners to reflect on the spiritual topography of their city. These writers each contribute one chapter of five thousand words on the place they live. This is spiritual geography and topographical exegesis, relative to spirituality, hope, change and transition, globalization, justice and civic design. How do these components together contribute to a social and spiritual imaginary? What impact on spiritual life does gentrification, immigration, and religious pluralism generate for urban Canadians? How have our relationships to our original peoples impacted the hope of shalom in urban life? How do these attitudes, ideologies, histories, and present forces impact the spiritual climate of a place?

The cities in focus are: Victoria, Vancouver, Kelowna, Calgary, Edmonton, Regina, Winnipeg, Ottawa, Toronto, Montreal, and Halifax. These cities were selected for their representative (wide) dispersion as well as by the location of appropriate contributors. Each contributes based on their own experience and expertise and their particular inhabitation of the place they live. Consequently, there are broad differences in the way they address the life of their city and its hopes and dreams, its failures and fears. As a collective we offer this book to you as a conversation on the rich spiritual geography of Canadian urban life today, in the hope of renewed and enriched engagement in the welfare of the peoples of Canada.

Hjalmarson

List of Contributors, from West to East

Professor Donald Goertz, Foreword

Dr. Leonard Hjalmarson, Introduction
Rob Crosby-Shearer, Victoria
Ross Lockhart, Vancouver
Paul Martinson, Kelowna
Dr. Cory Seibel, Edmonton
Dr. William McAlpine, Calgary
Spurgeon D. Root and Nick Helliwell, Regina
Jamie Howison, Winnipeg
Dr. James Watson, Toronto
Dr. Richard Long, Ottawa
Dr. Domenic Ruso, Montreal
Dr. Gary Thorne, Halifax

References

Campbell, Heidi A. & Garner, Stephen. (2016). *Networked Theology: Negotiating Faith in Digital Culture*. Grand Rapids: Baker Academic.

Carroll, Lewis. (1872). "*The Walrus and the Carpenter.*" In *Through the Looking Glass*. London: 1871.

Cronon, William. (1992). *Nature's Metropolis: Chicago and the Great West*. Chicago: WW Norton & Co.

The Eagles. (2003) In the City. Chicago: Warner Strategic.

Ellul, Jacques. (1970). *The Meaning of the City*. Grand Rapids: Eerdmans.

Hart, David Bentley. (2003). *The Beauty of the Infinite*. Grand Rapids: Eerdmans.

Hesiak, Jason. (2007, November 1). "Zizek and Evangelicals in America." Retrieved from http://churchandpomo.typepad.com/conversation/2007/11/zizek-and-evang.html

Keller, Tim. "The City." (2009). Retrieved from https://vimeo.com/3497788

Kostof, Spiro. (1991). *The City Shaped: Urban Patterns and Meanings Through History*. Oakland: Bullfinch Press.

Levenson, Jon D. (1985). *Sinai and Zion: An Entry into the Jewish Bible*. Minneapolis: Winston Press.

Lynch, Kevin. (1960). *The Image of the City*. Cambridge, MA: MIT Press.

Mercadante, Linda. (2004). Tasting the Bitter with the Sweet. In Kathryn Tanner (Ed.), *Spirit in the Cities (pp. 47-68)*, Minneapolis: Fortress Press.

Project for Public Spaces. (2012). "Creativity and Place-Making: Building Inspiring Centers of Culture." Retrieved from https://www.pps.org/reference/creativity-placemaking-building-inspiring-centers-of-culture/

Ramachandra, Vinoth. (2006, May 10). Christian Witness in an Age of Globalization. Leonard Buck Memorial Lecture, BCV, Melbourne.

Sheldrake, Philip. (2001). *Spaces for the Sacred*. Baltimore, MD: Johns Hopkins University Press.

Solnit, Rebecca. (2000). *Wanderlust: A History of Walking*. New York: Penguin Books.

Ward, Graham. (2005). Christian Political Practice and the Global City. *Journal of Theology for Southern Africa, 123*, 29-41.

_____. (2003). Why is the City So Important for Christian Theology?" *CrossCurrents*. 460-473.

Zizek, Slavoj. (1989).*The Sublime Object of Ideology*. London: Verso Books.

CHAPTER ONE
Victoria: An Imperfect Paradise

Rob Crosby-Shearer

As I write this, the most iconic symbol of the City of Victoria, BC is not the famed Empress Hotel (with its noted 'high tea'), nor is it the manicured Butchart Gardens north of the city, nor is it the Inner Harbour (with tall ships and a 41 million dollar yacht). The image that dominates the national news regarding Victoria is the homeless encampment, wedged between the nondescript Provincial Court building and the grand, towering neo-gothic edifice of Christ Church Anglican Cathedral in the city's downtown.

'Tent City' (known to its residents as "Super Intent City") – is an ironic triumph which has grown exponentially in the past year. It started as a few dozen homeless campers, tired of shelter shortages and being kicked out of parks at 7am (by-laws at least allow the homeless to camp there until then), while at the same time hoping to make a statement about the lack of provincial and federal support for housing. Since then, it has evolved into a mini-city-within-a-city; with infrastructure built of discarded shipping pallets, spare wood, tents, tarps, outhouses and even Wi-Fi access. It is decorated with spray painted banners and expressions of grassroots art.

Initially welcomed by the neighbouring Anglican Cathedral (and its private school) and with its presence defended by the Courts in a legal ruling, both the Cathedral and Courts have since moved to disavow themselves of this community of squatters. However one might view the politics and humanity of that situation, the Cathedral and the Courthouse can be seen as a microcosm of the landscape of this city, where the liberal elites of institutional Victoria, be they religious or civic, find themselves uncomfortably lifted above Tent City -- those very literally the marginalized, stuck there in the in-between.

When operating at its best, Tent City has developed a small, evolving democratic structure that happens in the form of regular meetings, which gathers residents together to talk about conflicts, hopes, ideals, safety, ideas and cares. Sometimes there are laments, prophetic critiques, and occasionally even prayers.

When I've attended the Tent City circle meetings, I've questioned the sustainability of this group in light of leadership issues, not to mention the pressure from both the inside and the outside. Over the months there have been very public issues of violence and drug abuse. Yet in spite of that, Tent City could be seen as a small piece of God's shalom in the love and hope that I've witnessed. I'm not sure how many of the folks who live there would identify as Christian (there are at least a few) but it sure does *feel* like 'church' in the best sense of the word: authentic, vulnerable, messy and hopeful.

Victoria, British Columbia is a town of paradoxes and contrasts.

Victoria was named, of course, after the 19th century British monarch. It is the capital of British Columbia, though it is often dwarfed in a myriad of ways by the much larger city of Vancouver, only 100 kilometres (a 1.5 hour ferry or short airplane ride) away. It is Canada's 15th largest municipality, but the actual city of Victoria, as opposed to the larger Greater Victoria region, only has a population of 80,000 people (more on this later).

In spite of being the legislative capital of the vast Province of BC, there is an almost mystifying sense of isolation in Victoria. Victorians do, after all, proudly live on an island, albeit a rather large one; some 460 km from top to the southern tip, where Victoria is situated. When it comes to culture, employment, food prices, and the like, that 100 km stretch of ocean is acutely felt. In spite of that, the political and ecclesial currents which come from the more culturally endowed lower mainland (i.e. Vancouver and environs) do affect Victorians.

Victoria is part of a larger bioregion known as "Cascadia"; an area that takes in the so-called "Pacific Northwest" of the USA as well as some of the Canadian lower mainland. Journalist Douglas Todd claims that, culturally speaking, this region is noted for "anti-institutional attitudes, often-bewildering ethnic pluralism, somewhat European sensibilities, liberal-left leanings... artistic and literary ties to a sacred sense of place" (Todd, 2008, p. 9).

I would posit that that's a pretty good description of Victoria as a whole, with the possible exception of ethnic pluralism, which, though present, is less diverse than Vancouver. Having said that, the more "Queen Victoria" (i.e. British, colonial) side of Victoria comes into tension with how Todd describes the region; and this tension resonates into many facets of life here.

Many of its residents refer to Vancouver Island (where Victoria is situated, not to be confused with the city of Vancouver) as 'paradise', a place of 'the good life'; and this is for good reason - at least in terms of weather. "We're like Vancouver here, but with less rain; we have green most of the year - and snow is rare," a local told me when I first moved here, proving largely correct.

Victoria is fast growing into a thriving tourist hub - and has become home to Canada's busiest cruise ship port-of-call, with 533,000 passengers welcomed during the 2015 season. (Greater Vancouver Harbour Authority, 2015). This changes life for residents, rich and poor alike - especially in the tourist season. In the last decade, Victoria's most-vulnerable residents have been gradually moved out of the tourist sections of town – and homeless shelters have been re-located in Rock Bay and further up Pandora Ave.

So, yes, there are shadows to this paradise.

Victoria was referred to as Canada's second most dangerous city (after Prince George, B.C.) in a 2010 Macleans' article (Macleans, 2010). Victorian apologists would note that the stats are skewed, since most so-called 'Victorians' (or those who consider themselves as such) live in the municipalities of Greater Victoria; those being Oak Bay, Saanich and Esquimalt. These areas are safer than "Victoria" proper, which has a much smaller population and more centralized social services and thus a higher crime rate.

There is a relatively large homeless population here, in part because of the milder weather. The Greater Victoria Coalition to End Homelessness notes that 1725 unique individuals used emergency beds in one of Victoria's shelters in 2014, and that was before there was a tent city; and this doesn't count those living in parks. 50% of those are identified as part of the Indigenous Community. That report also noted that Victoria is the second least affordable housing market in Canada, a situation which is intensifying as housing prices soar (Albert & Penner, 2015).

Year-round walks downtown in the very early mornings will find many people sleeping in doorways or in parks. The Mustard Street Church (Baptist); which also runs the foodbank for all of Vancouver Island, and Our Place (United Church) are two of the larger ecclesial responses. There is also a presence from the Salvation Army and smaller organizations such as the Dandelion Society and Street Hope – both grassroots efforts founded by Christians. Threshold Housing Society, which focuses on housing at-risk youth, housed 52 of the over 200 homeless youth in Victoria last year. Threshold was started as a response from parishioners to homeless youth hanging about the lawns of the Anglican Cathedral long before Tent City. There are also many important 'secular' advocacy groups, including the Cool Aid Housing Society and Pacifica Housing. There is some division between these groups, a tension intensified by the decision by the Provincial Government to bring in the Portland Hotel Society, a Vancouver-based non-profit to assist with the housing crisis.

In contrast to what I've thus far emphasized, the main public reputation of Victoria has, for decades, been "newlywed, nearly dead and garden beds" (so the popular phrase goes). There is still some element of truth to that. Again, one can take in the famed high tea ($75 / per person) at the Empress or casually wander at Butchart Gardens as enduring symbols of this culture and, yes, there are still many who move here to retire. However, as a recent Toronto Star article pointed out, this is rapidly changing as:

> . . . people in their 20s and 30s are moving here now, drawn by a booming tech sector. And the flock of retirees is getting younger — 50s are the 30s. Sure, you can still pick up a stack of Irish linens or get your age spots removed, but you can also pop into Smoking Lily for a periodic table silkscreened on a dress and find plenty of grooming shops for the ubiquitous gnome beards. (Alford, 2016)

So the web of human cultures in Victoria is exactly that – a diverse tapestry, shifting and complex, perhaps even more rapidly than other mid-sized Canadian cities. Add into that mix the provincial governmental culture, a booming University (and several other post-secondary educational institutions) and a relatively small space and population. All of this forms a compelling landscape within which to imagine God's vision of shalom breaking through in signs and symbols in this place.

* * *

When I moved here four years ago, I found it socially and economically difficult to adjust to life for our young family. I've had many conversations with younger folks, some who are professionals, who have confided that they are having a hard time making ends meet. Many of the parents at the school my kids attend work for minimum wage (currently $10.45 - the lowest in all of Canada's provinces). Many professionals that I know take on multiple jobs. For those who are more economically challenged, social housing is sought in order to make ends meet. In a town where skilled minimum wage jobs abound, the Greater Victoria Planning Council has noted that:

> ... the wage needed to cover the costs of raising a family in Greater Victoria is $20.05 per hour. This is the 2015 Greater Victoria living wage rate, the hourly wage that two working parents with two young children must earn to meet their basic expenses (including rent, child care, food and transportation), once government taxes, credits, deductions and subsidies have been taken into account. (Ross, 2015, 1)

Many younger folks are increasingly supported by parents, if not directly, then in other tangible ways such as child support or housing. Jobs in government and education are the main exceptions to low wages, but I am aware of people in those usually well-paid spheres who also struggle with Victoria's cost of living.

Victoria is a place of stunning natural environment. There's the ocean, the beaches, the mountains on the horizon, the network of bike trails, the lakes and trails. Even within the city one can't help notice the connection between the transcendent natural environment and the noted (post) secularity of the place. With the emphasis on recreation, it's not surprising that, statistically-speaking, relatively few Victorians engage traditional religion. If Victorians of European descent were to have a dominant religion, it is a religion of leisure, rooted in the natural environment, often blended with a vague and esoteric mix of new age sensibilities. Related to this, the 2011 National Household Survey notes that Greater Victoria has 146,000 Christians and then 172,000 who list as "No Religious Affiliation." (StatsCan, 2011).

A passing glance at a community board in one of the numerous coffee shops in this city will quickly give one the spiritual temperature here, where chakra belly dancing workshops hang alongside contemplative retreats. One could argue that the sheer number of these events betrays a collective longing for something that has been lost in the shift from traditional and collective religious forms (embodied in First Nations and Euro-Tribal/Christian traditions) to the more 'spiritual but not religious' mentality. James K.A. Smith (2014) summarizes the Canadian Roman Catholic philosopher Charles Taylor by saying that:

> . . . we live in a brass heaven, ensconced in immanence. We live in the twilight of both gods and idols. But their ghosts have refused to depart, and every once in a while we might be surprised to find ourselves tempted by belief, by intimations of transcendence... even as faith endures in the secular age, believing doesn't come easy. (p. 3-4)

Many of us on the West Coast engage these intimations of transcendence as our primary form of spirituality, though the echoes of older ways exist They persist in symbols such as our Christian architecture (whether the buildings remain in church use or not) or in the echoes of First Nations cultures which are ubiquitous, though they are effectively muted by the trauma of colonization.

A walk through downtown Victoria will find a plethora of diverse Christian symbols, some intact such as St. Andrew's Presbyterian, Glad Tidings Pentecostal, Central Baptist, Christ Church Cathedral, St. Andrew's RC Cathedral, First Met United – there are many more. Others are relegated to secular prominence, such as the Conservatory of Music, once a Methodist house of worship where Rev. Thomas Crosby, who I'll write about later, was ordained as a minister. In secular Victoria, many of these intact Christian institutions, whatever their theological stripe may be, are struggling to (re)determine their primal mission and find fiscal and communal sustainability.

In the downtown core, there are far fewer prominent symbols of First Nation's cultures, except on the Museum lawn. Historical pictures show Songhees and Esquimalt longhouses and ceremonies in the inner harbour and within the inner city. The long and painful legacy of colonialism, in which the mainstream Christian Churches played a willing role, has marginalized architectural expressions of First Nations spirituality to reserves, which sit well at the edges of the municipalities of Esquimalt, Saanich and Brentwood Bay.

The contrasts continue: The Anglican Cathedral, with its towering neo-gothic spires and the flags of fusiliers and the Hudson's Bay Company, feels like a haunted museum of such colonialism, with an occasional concert or tribute to the Queen. This at a time when Victoria's left-leaning Mayor Lisa Helps refuses to take the traditional vow of allegiance to the Queen, wanting instead to emphasize that Victoria is, in fact, the traditional lands of the Esquimalt and Songhees First Nations. It is a common West Coast practice, especially by mainstream civic, educational and religious organizations, to begin a time of gathering with an acknowledgement of the traditional lands of the First Nations who reside here. The painful ghost of colonialism is never distant.

For example, Mount Douglas, just north of the city, was named after a noted 19th century Governor who established the precursor to the Anglican Cathedral. Douglas had a mixed relationship with First Nations peoples, so that as a symbol the name cuts two ways. Thus the movement to change the mountain back to its traditional SENĆOŦEN name of PKOLS. Victoria is a place haunted by tradition, and particularly the tensions between Euro-Christian people and First Nations.

One of the great mythological Christian figures of Vancouver Island is the Rev. Thomas Crosby (1840-1914) – who called himself a 'missionary to the Indians [sic] of British Columbia'. In his book "Among the An-Ko-Me-Nums", he writes of a revival in 1872:

> The services at Victoria were first held on the reservation and then transferred to a building in the city which had been used as a bar-room. On a Sabbath morning in October '72 Elizabeth Deex, a chieftess of the Tsimshian nation... by the preaching of the Word was brought under deep conviction for sin... That meeting proved to be the beginning of a revival which lasted continuously for nine weeks and resulted in the conversion of upwards of forty natives. (Crosby, 1907, 235-236)

The story, sadly, goes on to tell that Crosby managed to alienate Deex, who became disillusioned by his racism – he passed over trained First Nations (Christian) teachers in favour of Caucasian ones - as well as Crosby's resistance to traditional First Nations ceremonies such as weddings and the Potlach.

The residential schools are the most explicit expression of this type of supremacist colonial attitude. Church and State partnered in an experiment to create 'good Christian Canadians' by removing First Nation's children from their home contexts and then systematically obliterating their culture, language and traditional ways. This history haunts the spiritual landscape of Victoria. The abuse experienced by First Nation peoples', often at the hands of Christian clergy, laity or religious continues to play out in the lives of First Peoples, as well as in the relationships between First Nations and settlers, especially Christians.

One can only wonder how different the relationships with First Nations and the secular landscape of Victoria might have been if Crosby and the other settler Christians had overcome their Euro-centric and racist impulses. As I ponder the possibility of shalom here, I can't help but wonder if it's not too late for reconciliation? Perhaps Victoria is now at a pivotal time for deepening relationships between the Euro-Tribal Churches and the First Peoples.

One of the bright lights in the spiritual landscape is the small attempts at such relationship building, many of which operate under the radar of the larger institutions and some of which come from their very heart. The current Anglican Bishop, the Right Rev. Dr. Logan McMenamie, recently walked from the north of Vancouver Island to Victoria, seeking forgiveness and reconciliation. I would posit that if there is hope for a deep, biblical sense of reconciliation then this relational work of listening, surrender and prayer, embodied in such a walk, must continue and deepen.

Victoria is a landscape of ecclesial, educational, cultural and civic fragmentation. Since this chapter is about the soul of the city, let's start with ecclesial fragmentation and move out from there.

The libertarian, anti-institutional frontier influence that Douglas Todd referred to makes Victorians a group of non-joiners. Even those who do join seem to keep splintering. Here, even the Unitarians have both a 'lay-led' congregation and a more 'traditional' clergy-led one.

My own 'tribe' of the Christian Church, the Anglican one, has been fragmenting for nearly a century and a half here. Anglicans have long considered ourselves able to hold in tension varying liturgical practices, theologies, and emphases. In Victoria we have Anglican Catholic, Traditional Anglican, and Anglican Network, all of whom splintered off of the more 'mainstream' Anglican Church of Canada. The issues varied: the ordination of women, a new prayer book, or recently issues surrounding the inclusion of LGBTQ+ persons.

The first splinter happened here in Victoria back with the so-called Schism of 1874 – when Dean Edward Cridge, then of the Anglican

Cathedral, led an evangelical 'low church' walk-out and subsequently built Church of Our Lord down the hill. The United Church of Canada held its most divisive national General Council in Victoria in 1988 – where they affirmed a commitment to the inclusion of LGBTQ+ people at all levels of that Church, including clergy. Shortly afterward, many of the evangelical and charismatic United Churches split off, joining other evangelical churches or, alternately, starting splinter denominations.

As mainstream churches split and schism there are over 30 relatively-new Church Plants in Greater Victoria; a large number given the population base. Many of these are from these splinter groups of Baptists, Presbyterians, Pentecostals, Anglicans, Congregationalists (United), Reformed and Mennonite groupings, all of whom feel that the established versions of these Christian traditions aren't engaging secular Cascadian culture enough and are resting on their laurels as they decline.

The famous Canadian Painter, Emily Carr, early in her life attended Church of Our Lord (the Anglican Cathedral split-off) as well as a Presbyterian Church, before then becoming a Methodist (even then Victorians were non-joiners, I guess!). She wrote this in "The Book of Small": "The little Church [Church of our Lord] smiled up from the mud flats, the Cathedral frowned down, austere and national, and Victorians chose high or low, whichever comforted them the most." (Carr, 2004. p. 112)

Over one hundred years later, at least for those who have that privilege of choice, it seems that little has changed.

Shifting to education for a moment, Victoria's education systems reflect a similar tendency to division and fragmentation. There are a good number of elite, British-style private schools, religious schools, and specialty schools catering to the eco-conscious or the Montessori impulse, as examples. There is, as in much of Canada, a public school system; which itself has divisions between 'traditional' schools, conventional and French immersion streams. Some parents, especially those coming out of either ecological or evangelical Christian culture (or both, in some cases) follow the more libertarian 'do-it-yourself' Cascadian impulse and lean towards homeschooling.

My own experience from working in youth ministry is that the cultural and economic separatism between the various private and public systems (and home schoolers) creates an economically two (or more) tiered system in Victoria, which in many ways mirrors the fragmentation that I've spoken about in the Churches.

One final anecdote on fragmentation: I once made a comment to a long-time resident about the lack of cultural diversity in Victoria. She replied: "You've never shopped at Wal-Mart, have you?" She was right. To another friend I made a similar quip. Her response: "Unless you ride the bus, of course" (Crosby-Shearer, Private Conversation, 2015). When I do ride the bus, or shop at Wal-Mart, the visible population of South Asian, South East Asian, Black Canadians, African and Caribbean Canadians, and First Nations people becomes more evident. The influx of Syrian Refugees, many sponsored by the Churches, Mosques and Synagogues (sometimes together) is also changing the landscape.

How is it, then, that where we shop, where we go to school, where we go to church and which forms of transport we take divide us so much in Victoria? This is an important question to explore if we're to examine the soul of this city.

When one looks at Victoria, one has to consider that the fragmentation I've noted is not just ecclesial or educational, but is also civic. Because it's built on the tip of an island, Victoria can be a confusing place for those more used to the North American grid mentality of streets. To add to the confusion, the streets seem to change names every few blocks in Victoria and Greater Victoria. Then consider that when an outsider thinks about "Victoria," one is likely thinking of several different political municipalities: Victoria, Saanich, Oak Bay and Esquimalt.

As I've already noted, Victoria itself has a relatively small population of about 80,000 people – while Greater Victoria has a population of nearly 345,000 in the four geographically close municipalities. Looking even wider the area comprises 13 municipalities which take in the far southern part of Vancouver Island, albeit still with only 370,000 residents in total.

The municipalities of Greater Victoria have resisted amalgamation. This could be viewed negatively as a product of insularity and parochialism, or of that individualist libertarian spirit. However, when looking toward a vision of shalom, bucking the conservative trend toward becoming a larger entity has allowed for greater diversity, including a distinct 'small town' feel to each of the areas. Neighbourhoods within these smaller municipalities have retained some of their life-giving characteristics. Indeed, a more 'micro-urban' mentality should not be written off, as within the small area of Victoria municipality are over a dozen distinct neighbourhoods.

The point of this chapter isn't merely to describe the city -- its struggles and its hopes – but to paint some kind of picture of how it acts as a sign of the in-breaking Kingdom of God. I've already alluded to this fragile hope in the situation at Tent City, where homeless have taken it upon themselves to organize and advocate in a way that larger society wouldn't. I've alluded to it in the diverse tapestry of cultures. And I've identified some of the barriers resulting from fragmentation, especially those based on the intersections of ethnicity, culture, economics and religion.

If that's the big picture, I'd now like to narrow the lens and focus on my own neighbourhood of Fernwood, where the Church plant and neo-monastic community that I'm part of is located. What are the possibilities for a Biblical vision of shalom?

The diversity of housing in Fernwood includes an array of single-family homes, rental units within houses, apartment blocks, co-operatives, co-housing, social housing, and neighbourhood-created housing. The city by-law allowing homeless residents to camp in parks between 8pm until 7am further diversifies Fernwood, given the relatively close walking proximity to the various social services downtown.

Fernwood has been home to many initiatives and projects to make it a better place, many of them emerging from the grassroots. There's a permaculture garden (the Spring Ridge Commons), a Compost Education Centre, a community well dug from the old spring, numerous neighbourhood and street festivals and even two neighbourhood groups with varying emphases (this might be a new tribalism, or part of those historical fragmentations). More informally, Fernwood is known as a place where there is a culture of leaving old 'stuff' on the curb. Moving day is a great day in Fernwood to scavenge just about anything: an inborn commitment to a culture of grassroots recycling and reusing.

Decades ago, the old village centre in Fernwood, once the turn-around loop for the streetcars from downtown, was fairly run-down and even considered dangerous. The community banded together to reclaim the decrepit buildings and, with the support of famed Canadian environmentalist David Suzuki, put in a café, affordable housing, a community centre and several garden initiatives.

The abandoned church was converted into a theatre. Another industrial space became home to the Paul Phillip's theatre, where the church plant I am part of currently meets. (which is ironic, given that the space was the supply and office depot for the contractors who built the Anglican Cathedral).

The Soul of the City

Graffiti, usually in the form of gang tagging, was an issue in the neighbourhood. Rather than fight the gangs, the residents decided to have a pole painting day every year. Noting that there was an unspoken 'code' amongst the taggers, that they considered what they did art, and would not tag over other art. When the city made boulevard gardens legal as a pilot project, many in Fernwood expanded their capacity to grow food, as well as to beautify, with ornamental plants expanding to their boulevards.

With all that I've mentioned, there certainly is some gentrification happening, as Fernwood has become a more and more 'desirable' neighbourhood to live in. However, the diversity of the housing in Fernwood, bolstered by a community spirit, has kept much of the socio-economic diversity intact.

Interestingly, the church broadly (institutionally) has had little role in the positive transformations. The former Emmanuel Baptist left for the suburbs and its vacated building is now the Belfry Theatre, after a stint as a Cool Aid housing shelter. The former Belmont United Church now houses a ballet studio and the Shambhala Meditation Centre. St. Alban's Anglican was sold in 2011, in spite of the protests of neighbourhood groups, and replaced with higher-end housing. The Lutheran Church is now a music store. The former Traditional Anglican Church (an Orange hall and a Unitarian Church before that) has become private housing which was recently made-over and sold for 1.2 million dollars.

But it wasn't always this way. There is a plaque in the park by the Fernwood Community Centre noting the work of the Rev. William Stevenson, whom the park is named after. The plaque notes Stevenson's presence in the neighbourhood at the turn of the (nineteenth) century as pastor of Emmanuel Baptist, noting his work with neighbourhood youth.

Another plaque speaks of a Presbyterian schoolteacher who would march her poorer students downtown to buy shoes for them.

When we in the missional Church / local Church / parish Church movements speak about 'coming alongside what God is doing in the neighbourhood' – it seems to me that we have a whole lot of catching up to do. There is something humbling, though distressing about that.

And the changes aren't without their struggles. While Fernwood is still considered amongst 'old-timers' as slightly 'dangerous,' there is a yoga studio, an upscale café, a wine bar and an upscale children's clothing store in Fernwood Square. Some homeless folks have been moved from sleeping in certain parks and green spaces. The abandoned buildings and tagged poles have been transformed into a progressive hub of street parties and community initiatives. And this is good, but with a caveat. The coming of God's kingdom and creation of a place where everyone can live beneath their vine and fig tree is great – but it must not be confused with blatant gentrification in Fernwood, where the line between those two rests is uncertain.

In spite of the diversity of housing, there are troubling signs. The 2-bedroom bungalow across the street, which was listed for $800,000 Canadian dollars sold for $920,000 – with over 20 offers – most without any conditions, according to a realtor friend of mine. "Folks selling their houses in Vancouver for 1.5 million and getting a real bargain here in a quieter town" one person noted to me. The cultural and economic waves from across the water are affecting us, emphasizing our interrelationship even with those distant from Vancouver Island. Housing has become such a hot commodity that many people bring their inspectors along to viewings to avoid having any conditions.

* * *

Tent City is about a 15-minute walk from Fernwood. As I conclude this chapter, Tent City is being dismantled by order of the

Province. Graciously, there has been no visible confrontations that I've heard of. Many have left of their own accord. A friend of mine who is a social worker and has spent a lot of time down there, sent me a note saying he walked through and his heart broke. Another friend, a parishioner at the Anglican Cathedral, helped to organize an all-day prayer vigil at the Cathedral for Tent City.

Perhaps these responses demonstrate that, for all the platitudes and brokenness in our relationships and situations, sometimes the only way we can begin to perceive the Shalom of God is to lament and get on our knees.

A few weeks back, I walked past the soon-to-be dismantled Tent City. There were two large, spray-painted banners at the North-West Corner, facing the Cathedral. Both in bold letters, the two signs offered differing sentiments.

> One read: "SOCIAL HOUSING NOW. INDEPENDENT CAMPS / BUILDINGS"
> The other, obviously paraphrasing St. Paul, said this:
> > LOVE IS PATIENT, KIND, ENDURING
> > LOVE ISN'T SELFISH, JEALOUS
> > LOVE DOESN'T: PROVOKE, BEGRUDGE
> > LOVE IS ALL WE NEED. IT IS IMPERFECT.
> > TRUST LOVE. EVEN ALONE, IT HEALS.
> > LOVE WILL ALWAYS PREVAIL.

As I dream about this city and its potential to embody God's reign, I hope that what I've presented here isn't too negative. I love this place, but I recognize that if there's any truth that resurrection (and thus Kingdom) emerges from the brokenness of crucifixion, then all the stories -- both the hopes and the shadows -- represent God's redeeming work. It's a messy beauty that I've witnessed here.

Victoria, though paradise in so many ways, is a very broken, imperfect paradise. With the contrasts, shifts, contradictions and fragments I've chronicled, how can God's people live more deeply and prayerfully into that Biblical vision of shalom? What does it mean to be Church in this context? How might Christians partner with others of good will (even amidst the fragments) to hold the beautiful, creative tension of what God is already doing through the Holy Spirit?

How could that movement of the Spirit, the movement to the great reconciliation of God's reign of justice, shalom and joy reverberate outward to all of greater Victoria and to all of God's beloved, blessed and broken creation?

References

Albert, Marika & Penner, T. (2015). Homelessness in Greater Victoria. *Victoria: Greater Victoria Coalition to End Homelessness*. Retrieved from http://victoriahomelessness.ca/wp-content/uploads/2015/12/2014-15_RHS_FINAL.pdf

Alford, Jennifer. (2016, April 16). Cool Victoria Is No Longer Just for the 'Newlywed and Nearly Dead.' *The Star*. Retrieved from https://www.thestar.com/life/travel/2016/04/03/cool-victoria-is-no-longer-just-for-the-newlywed-and-nearly-dead.html

Macleans. (2010). Canada's Most Dangerous Cities: 2010. *Macleans*. Retrieved from http://www.macleans.ca/news/canada/national-crime-rankings-2010/

Carr, Emily. (2004). *The Book of Small*. Vancouver: Douglas and McIntire, 2004.

Crosby, Thomas. (1907). *Among the An-ko-me-nums or Flathead tribes of Indians of the Pacific Coast*. Toronto: W. Briggs. Retrieved from: https://archive.org/details/amongankomenums000cros

Greater Victoria Harbour Authority. (2015). Cruise. Retrieved from http://www.gvha.ca/ogden-point-terminal/cruise

Macleans. (2010). Canada's Most Dangerous Cities: 2010. *Macleans*. Retrieved from http://www.macleans.ca/news/canada/national-crime-rankings-2010/

Smith, James K.A. (2014). *How (Not) To Be Secular: Reading Charles Taylor*. Grand Rapids: Eerdmans.

Statistics Canada. (2011). Religion, Immigrant Status, and Period of Immigration, Age Groups and Sex for the Population in Private Households. Retrieved from http://www.statcan.gc.ca/eng/help/bb/info/religion

Ross, Mary Katherine. (2015, April 29). Living wage rises again in 2015. *Community Social Planning Council*. Retrieved from http://www.communitycouncil.ca/sites/default/files/2015_April_29_Living_Wage_Calculation_Release.pdf

Todd, Douglas, ed. (2008). *Cascadia The Elusive Utopia. Exploring the Spirit of the Pacific Northwest*. Vancouver: Ronsdale Press.

Hjalmarson

CHAPTER TWO

Vancouver, BC

Ross Lockhart

My secret is that I need God – that I am sick and can no longer make it alone."

- Douglas Coupland, Life After God

It's early on a dark, damp winter morning at the base of Grouse Mountain. I stand across the street from a row of townhouses that our family of five calls home, waiting for the #247 TransLink bus to downtown Vancouver. Above me, through the gentle rain, I can see the snow covered peaks of nearby mountains and my nostrils fill with the rich and textured scent of thousand year old cedar trees in the forest nearby. Every day as I leave our Canyon Heights neighbourhood, tourists flow the opposite direction to visit Vancouver's best-known attractions including Cleveland Dam, Grouse Mountain and the Capilano Suspension Bridge. Vancouverite Douglas Coupland describes this area where I wait for my bus in a way reminiscent of Celtic Christians, who spoke of thin places where heaven and earth kissed. Coupland says of the Grouse Mountain neighbourhood, "the air is thin, the view is spectacular, and the presence of something holy is always just a breath and a glance away, off in the hinterlands" (Coupland, 2000, p. 92).

This day and everyday, the same assortment of professionals line up to catch the early bus downtown. As always, these Vancouverites maintain a cool distance from each other and yet, oddly, when the journey is finished everyone will go out of their way to say "thank you" to the unknown bus driver, a move that would raise eyebrows in other Canadian cities. My daily commute as a pastor and professor at St. Andrew's Hall on the University of British Columbia (UBC) campus, takes me down from North Vancouver, across the Capilano river to West Vancouver, with the wealthiest postal codes in Canada - where homes sell for up to thirty million dollars.10 From there I cross the iconic Lion's Gate Bridge through Stanley Park and into the bustling downtown core. On the journey, snow-covered mountains of stone give way to sparkling condo towers of steel and glass. Here I say, "thank you" to the bus driver, cross the street and stand for a few minutes waiting to take the #44 bus to UBC.

As I wait, the sights, sounds and smells of my surroundings could not be more different than where the journey began twenty minutes earlier on the mountainside of North Vancouver. Vancouver is known by many nicknames including "wet city, Lotusland, Vangroovy, and Hollywood North," but Douglas Coupland's description of "City of Glass" fits best. You know it when you stand downtown surrounded by countless high-rises, shimmering and reflecting the lights and sights of the city in the walls of glass condominiums and office towers. Here, the urban core of Canada's third largest city is on display for all to see, with bustling crowds and a dizzying dichotomy of wealth and poverty. I wait on Burrard Street for my next bus and nearby me sleeps a homeless man, bundled in soiled (formerly) white blankets trying to escape the cold of the winter rain. He leans his malnourished and bruised body against the outside of the newly renovated Tiffany's jewelry store. On the other side of me a dark, sleek Maserati sports car (starting price - $100,000) speeds by dangerously close to the curb, blasting through a puddle that sends a

---

10 A check of real estate listings in August 2017 had 145 homes for sale in the Greater Vancouver area at 10 million dollars or higher. Retrieved from https://www.realtor.ca/Residential/

The Soul of the City

spray up towards those of us traveling on the cheap. As we scatter out of the way, the water hits the front of the Tiffany store and drips down on the unfortunate soul trying to sleep through the morning commute.

Not far behind the Maserati, we witness a Bentley (starting price $180,000). It slows down to a more reasonable speed, stopping in front of our passenger queue, all of us now on alert for splashing water. The Bentley blocks the bus stop as a man in a high quality suit steps out. With a leather briefcase in hand, the businessman nods to the driver before pushing his way through the crowd waiting for the bus. A horn sounds. The #44 TransLink vehicle has appeared and is impatiently waiting behind the Bentley, the bus driver's face contorted in anger as he gestures to the luxury car to get out of his space.

Once on the #44 bus we move through downtown Vancouver, passing more tall glass condo towers, seeded with a smattering of low-rise heritage buildings. Crossing over the Art Deco Burrard Street Bridge, tall electronic billboards advertise the latest in consumer needs, the signs owned by the Squamish First Nations on land reclaimed in the heart of the city they once called home. The bus moves through the leafy green neighbourhoods of Kitsilano, home to Lululemon and West Point Grey where "students" own multimillion-dollar homes instead of living in residence. We cross through the University Endowment Lands, that unmistakable greenbelt that separates the city from The University of British Columbia. Here, we leave the City of Vancouver and enter a separate quasi municipality where the highest authority for landowners and residents is the UBC Senate. The campus swirls with life as students, staff and faculty move helter-skelter off to class or research. A cacophony of babel-like voices rise above the crowd, high up into the slowly clearing blue sky, the sky mirrored off the ocean waves.

Vancouver takes its name from an Englishman in the Royal Navy;

Captain George Vancouver first visited the deep harbours of this region and exchanged greetings with Indigenous peoples in 1792, a year after the Spanish first dropped anchor in the area. Settlement of the territory began in earnest thirty-five years later with the establishment of Fort Langley in 1827. New Westminster, now a suburb of Vancouver, was the first urban area developed on the banks of the British Columbia's longest river (over 1,300 kilometers), named for the Northwest Company's famous explorer Simon Fraser. New Westminster became firmly established during the famous Fraser River gold rush (1858-1863) when a flood of prospectors, mostly American, moved through the region on their way north seeking fame and fortune. The two separate British colonies of Vancouver Island and mainland British Columbia were united in 1866 with New Westminster as the capital. The arrangement lasted for two years until the more established city of Victoria (dating back to 1843) won out as the seat of government. By Confederation in 1867 conversation turned to joining the other British colonies stretched across British North America.

Finally conditions were set, including the need for a national railway system to link east and west, and the majority of male, British, non-indigenous citizens who were permitted to vote, voted to join Confederation in 1871. The railway would take another fifteen years to finally reach the west coast, but when it did arrive the City of Vancouver took on new geometry as the Canadian Pacific Railroad found the Gastown area a better harbor and terminus for shipping than the original Port Moody site. 1886 marked the founding of the City of Vancouver. However, by the beginning of the 20th Century Victoria and Vancouver were actually similar in size. Throughout the 20th century, with the rise of urbanization, centralization of wealth from the resource based economy and post Second World War boom, Vancouver outstripped Victoria as the major city in the province. The city never looked back.

Expo 86, with its theme of technology and communications drew an astounding twenty-two million visitors from across North America and around the world. It was my first trip to Vancouver and the mild west coast climate, stunning natural aesthetics and modern cityscape (not to mention the adorable Expo Ernie robot!) left an impression that would later draw many of us back as residents and citizens in this "City of Glass." Greater Vancouver is a cosmopolitan, world class city that has grown to a population of 2,463,431 in 2016. It is renowned for natural beauty, diverse ethnic culture and access to world-class recreation facilities in places like Squamish and Whistler (Vancouver Census Profile, 2016).

Beauty is said to be skin deep, however, so we need to probe this west coast urban centre and ask what lies beneath the surface. When I spoke with a mentor, Stephen Farris, then Dean at St. Andrew's Hall where I now work, and told him that my family was moving to the west coast to pastor a local congregation he offered some advice. "Congratulations. Welcome to paradise. I know you grew up on the prairies and you're moving from Ontario after ministering in the Maritimes, but don't think of moving to Vancouver like anywhere else you've been in Canada. Think of moving to British Columbia like emigrating to a new country." In many ways, it was the best advice I ever received before moving to the west coast.

As a Canadian, the moment you land in Vancouver you recognize that the geography, climate and culture are different here than the rest of the country. The soaring, tree-lined, snow capped mountains sweep down majestically to the sparkling ocean in postcard perfection. Vegetation is different here, thriving year round in hues of deep green, with vibrant tropical flowers. Palm trees sway in the wind, pointing west towards Hawaii or south to California. The influence of Asian culture is especially strong, with 43% of the local population claiming Asian heritage, making Vancouver the "most Asian city outside of Asia" (Todd, 2014). Health and fitness are prized by the locals, with year round activity: from yoga in the park to skiing on the North Shore Mountains to cycling the city's designated bike lanes. Even octogenarians are wearing Lululemon and sipping lattes while strolling the seawall. And while I've often said that the "hardest thing about preaching heaven in Vancouver is people think they're already there;" a shadow side to this west coast paradise lurks just beneath the surface.

Economic disparity in the region is striking. Housing is a major social issue impacting quality of life for residents, with Vancouver ranked the third most expensive city in the world, trailing only Sydney, Australia and Hong Kong (Hayward, 2017). The average price of a detached home in Vancouver ranges between 1.6 and 1.8 million dollars (Jang, 2017). At $11.35 an hour, Vancouverites have to live in the third most expensive city in the world with one of the lowest minimum wages in the country. "When workers are last in the country, in the most expensive province in the country, our government has to do something about that," B.C. Federation of Labour President Irene Lanzinger cautioned recently (Zussman, 2016).

When you dig deeper into the economic crisis here in Vancouver you encounter the prickly issue of money flooding the market from overseas: foreign investment. The Vancouver Sun profiled the majority owner of a Point Grey mansion that was sold by Canaccord founder Peter Brown for a record $31.1 million to a "student." Land title documents list Tian Yu Zhou as having a 99-per-cent interest in the five-bedroom, eight-bathroom, 14,600 square-foot mansion on a 1.7-acre lot at 4833 Belmont Ave. Zhou's occupation is listed as a "student" (Olivier, 2016). That's a bit larger than the dorm rooms I remember in university! Stories like this have angered locals, frustrated with the lack of affordability. Mount Pleasant resident Eveline Xia took to Twitter to express her anger at the city's housing crisis. Xia started #DontHave1Million to protest home prices, as Statistics Canada data shows a net loss of residents aged 20 to 30 years old from the Vancouver area, with Millennials seeking affordable pastures across the country. (Jackson, 2015).

Of course, the growing gap between rich and poor in the city is not just an economic question, but a spiritual one as well. Vancouver is famous for being home to Canada's wealthiest postal code (West Vancouver) and Canada's poorest (Downtown Eastside Vancouver). As Douglas Coupland (2000) described the odd reality, "Heroin is a given. The corner of Main and Hastings is in the poorest postal code in Canada and is home to untold social ills, not the least of which is smack. Adding to its weirdness is its close proximity to perky, cruise-liner friendly Gastown, and to fastidious Chinatown." The disparity between rich and poor in this west coast city raises questions about our idol making and captivity to wealth and privilege. As Soong-Chan Rah (2009) argues, "Materialism and consumerism reduced people to a commodity. An individual's worth in society is based upon what assets they bring and what possessions they own...we begin to believe that our spiritual problems can be solved with material goods." (p. 49).

For Vancouverites who self identify as people of faith, the economic tension in the city is especially problematic. Theologically, following Jesus in a culture of North American affluence "either by enjoying economic prosperity or buying into the culture assumption that everyone aspires to be affluent" presents multiple challenges. (Lockhart, 2016, xxiv). The Parish Collective in nearby Seattle identify these challenges when they argue,

Economics functions as a mirror, where the truth about your faith is reflected back. The spreadsheet is a theological statement, reflecting any incongruence between what you say you believe and how you steward your resources. This reality can be painful. The close connection of economics to the practicing of your faith is reflected in the simple principle that Jesus communicated: 'Where your treasure is, there your heart will be also....' To think of faith and economics primarily in terms of philanthropic giving is to fundamentally mistake what economics are and why they are so powerful. At a core level economics has to do with basic exchange, receiving and giving. This exchange is behind common word pairings such as spending and earning, investing and accruing, or borrowing and lending. The connection between your treasure and your heart is not simply about how you give; it's also about how you earn, which means there is nothing that has to do with money that doesn't have to do with your heart. Your heart is connected to your treasure. (Sparks, 2014, p. 97-98)

In this culture of affluence, Christian leaders in Vancouver must recognize the need for the Gospel story to trump the narratives of consumerism and materialism all around. Richard Bauckham asks in Bible and Mission what the church needs in order to recognize and resist the metanarrative of unfettered capitalism and globalization. He responds, "Surely a story that counters the global dominance of the profit-motive and the culture of consumption with a powerful affirmation of the universal values? But the Christian metanarrative can adopt this role only if it resists becoming a tool of the force of domination. (Bauckham, 2003, p. 97)

Perhaps part of the reason Vancouver has turned out this way is it's historic self-identification with rugged individualism. People move here from other places to escape commitments to social or religious institutions. As a friend of mine said lately over a chai latte, "Vancouverites are not joiners. They'll commit to a short-term running club or something, but don't ask them to get involved in a long-term voluntary organization. That will just freak them out." There is a shadow side to this rugged individualism. In its well-researched, detailed and thoughtful 2012 report, the Vancouver Foundation released its findings regarding social isolation for residents entitled, "Connections and Engagement." The Foundation funded research that included interviews with 3,841 local citizens of over 80 different ethnic groups as well as 275 non-profit organizations and 100 notable community leaders. The research discovered that:

> Metro Vancouver can be a hard place to make friends
>
> One-third of the people...surveyed say it is difficult to make new friends here. And one in four say they are alone more often than they would like to be. In both cases, people who experience this also report poorer health, lower trust and a hardening of attitudes toward other community members. (Vancouver Foundation, 2012, 7)
>
> Our neighbourhood connections are cordial, but weak
>
> While most of us know the names of at least two of our neighbours, the connections typically stop there. Most of us do not do simple favours for our neighbours (like taking care of their mail when they are away) and fewer have visited a neighbour's home or invited a neighbour over. One-third of the people we surveyed do not know if their neighbours trust each other. And barely a majority thinks that the ties in their neighbourhood are growing stronger. (Vancouver Foundation, 2012, 7)
>
> Many people in metro Vancouver are retreating from community life
>
> It isn't a lack of time that stops people from getting involved. The most often-cited reason for not participating in neighbourhood and community life is a feeling that we have little to offer.

> There are limits to how people see diversity as an opportunity to forge meaningful connections.
>
> Over one-third of us have no close friends outside our own ethnic group. And we generally believe that people prefer to be with others of the same ethnicity. Many people believe all new immigrants and refugees, regardless of where they come from, would be welcome in their neighbourhood. However, some residents rank which groups they believe would be the most and the least welcome. (Vancouver Foundation, 2012, 7)
>
> The affordability issue in metro Vancouver is affecting people's attitudes and beliefs.
>
> Most people believe Vancouver is becoming a resort town for the wealthy. These same people also tend to think that there is too much foreign ownership of real estate. (Vancouver Foundation, 2012, 7).

The report was eye opening for many in Vancouver who considered this Pacific Northwest community a friendly city made up of distinct neighbourhoods with character and culture. The glue that seems to hold a community together appears to be missing in Vancouver.

Traditionally, Christianity was one "bottle of glue" that helped form community cohesiveness in Canadian villages, towns and cities as franchises of Western Christendom set up shop in the British, French and Spanish colonies of North America. After all, it is Christianity that returns again and again to the question of Luke 10: 29, "Who is my neighbour?" But here in the Pacific Northwest, or Cascadia,[11] some argue that Christendom was never fully established. In her excellent work The Secular Northwest, historian Tina Block (2017) reminds us that census data today on both sides of the border indicate that "no religion"

---

[11] A term used to describe the shared geographic, social, and cultural values of the Pacific Northwest region that includes Oregon, Washington State and British Columbia.

is now the number one religion in the region (p. 2).12 Block's (2017) historical survey of faith in Cascadia found that, "Northwest secularity is most evident in the region's strikingly low levels of involvement in, and attachment to, formal or organized religion" (p. 48). Angus Reid's (2017) latest polling on religion in Canada confirms that B.C. is home to the highest proportion of Non-Believers at just over one-quarter (27%).

If Christendom unraveled most quickly here on the west coast due to the shallow roots of a Constantinian baptized social structure, then one must ask, "What kind of belief system has replaced traditional religion" in this "spiritual not religious" landscape of steel and glass? In his book Cascadia, Douglas Todd suggests that environmentalism or care for creation is essentially the civil religion of the Pacific Northwest. While people may not feel a bond to each other as closely here in Vancouver as they might to neighbours "back east," there is a close bond with nature and human beings' responsible care for it. When the new Student Union Building opened two years ago at The University of British Columbia, my colleague Jason Byassee and I wandered over for lunch. At the end of our sushi and carrot juice meal, we gathered our garbage and stood, trays in hand, before a dazzling array of choices. Separate recycling options were offered for chopsticks and plastics and cans and compost and a million other things before one would finally surrender and put anything in the "garbage." "Whoa," I said, "you don't want to get this wrong or you'll be a social pariah around here." "Man, we never had this kind of dilemma in North Carolina," replied Jason. Environmentalism has become the new civic religion on the West Coast (Lockhart, 2016).

Of course, there are positive aspects in Vancouver's environmentalism, such as the values it shares with the region's

---

12In her scholarly treatment of religion in Cascadia, Block argues that historically, "Northwesterners were part of a regional culture that placed relatively little importance on formal religious connections."

indigenous peoples. The Vancouver area is home to Squamish, Musqueam and Tsleil-Waututh First Nations, members of the Coast Salish linguistic group. Indigenous culture is celebrated in Vancouver from the moment you land at YVR and see the beautiful totems and welcoming figures carved from west coast cedar. Public events naturally include representatives of local First Nations, greeting, speaking, and even praying before other dignitaries. I recall a public assembly for our children's primary school that included speakers from the local Squamish nation to officially bless an addition to the school. I leaned over and reminded my wife of our time in Northern Ontario many years earlier, when opening ceremonies for a new firehall or other public space would include an invitation for me, as the token Protestant pastor in town, to speak and offer a blessing. Not in Vancouver. Not at the end of Christendom.

And neither is this only a "secular" phenomenon. Many churches have followed community organizations and now begin their meetings by declaring that they are on the traditional, ancestral and unceded territory of the Squamish or Musqueum peoples. The "unceded" part is especially important, as a unique reality of the Indigenous peoples here on the west coast. Local First Nations never signed treaties with the British Crown (unlike the rest of Canada) and therefore are in a much stronger position to negotiate for land and other resources needed to care for their people in 21st Century Canada.

The Christian community in Vancouver is especially mindful of the mainline denominations' partnership with the Federal government in the Residential Schools program in the 19th and 20th Century. This program of corporate and individual sin led representatives of Christ, in co-operation with the government, to seize Indigenous children from their homes and strip them of their culture in order to westernize the

First Nations. This unholy action of racial discrimination and cultural destruction was often accompanied by horrifying acts of physical and sexual abuse. The cross-country Truth and Reconciliation Commission (2016), and its subsequent report, helped highlight for a broader Canadian public the dangers of what Christianity wedded with State power can do to its own citizens.

As a result, Christianity looks and feels different here in Vancouver than other parts of North America. Christians operate mindful that they are a minority in the greater population, and yet they are mercifully free from the Christendom expectations of what Christian community must look and act like. Instead, there are remarkable examples of healthy, thriving Christian witnessing communities in Vancouver ranging from large churches like 10th Avenue, Willingdon, Coastal and West Side Church right down to smaller, vibrant neighbourhood churches like Grandview Calvary Baptist or Nelson Avenue Community Church, each engaging newcomers to Canada as well as post-Christian residents in their neighbourhoods. Church plants like St. Peter's Fireside through Tim Keller's Redeemer City-to-City network are establishing a strong, creative and vital orthodox Christian presence in the downtown core while connecting with young professionals seeking meaning in the midst of a cosmopolitan city of glass.

Often the visible growth of the Christian church in Vancouver is in alignment with larger social change factors such as immigration. For example, Tapestry Church was a "replanting" initiative of the local Classis that brought in Albert Chu from the Canadian and Missionary Alliance Church to begin a new ministry to Asian Canadians living in Richmond. They planted the new congregation within First Christian Reformed Church in Richmond as it was declining in numbers and represented the older, Euro-stock demographic of Richmond.

Richmond today is a community that bears the beautiful mark of diversity more than most mid-sized cities in Canada. In the 2011 National Household Survey, Statistics Canada reported that 133,320 individuals living in Richmond (where YVR – the Vancouver International Airport is located) out of a total of 189,305 residents belonged to a visible minority group, accounting for 70.4% of the community's total population (City of Richmond, 2011).

At a recent meeting of our Presbytery, Pastor Chu spoke to us as Presbyterians about both the faithful success of their ministry (now growing to multiple church plants throughout the region) as well as the resistance they encountered from within the existing church as an older Euro-tribal congregation declined and a new expression of the Body of Christ was birthed by the Holy Spirit. Indeed, the change in ethnic composition of the church and community exposes the darker side of humanity or, as we say as Presbyterians – human depravity.

Recently, Rev. Victor Kim of Richmond Presbyterian Church organized a rally at City Hall with other faith leaders in response to racist flyers circulated around the city. The posters produced by an "Alt Right" group against Chinese residents, prompted Rev. Kim to organize an open letter in response with eighteen other churches of various denominations and members of the wider multifaith community. Rev. Kim said, "We're living in some tenuous times where people feel like they've been given some license that they haven't always had....This is a time where how we respond to things will be a good example for the Lower Mainland and all of Canada" (Schaefer, 2016).

Signs of God's activity in post-Christendom Cascadia are not just evident in Protestant witnessing communities but Roman Catholic as well. The Catholic Archdiocese of Vancouver is growing in key parishes, due in large part to immigration, such as St. Patrick's parish in east

Vancouver (originally built by Irish immigrants and now predominately Filipino), St. Mary's Joyce Street that averages 7500 a week (also predominately Filipino), or St. Andrew Kim Church (in nearby Surrey with 3,000 weekly worshippers, most of whom are Korean).

Investigating the surge in Roman Catholic strength in so called "secular Vancouver" Jason Byassee (2016) reports that while immigration is a major factor,

> good old fashioned pastoral work is essential too (lots of churches fumble away natural advantages like immigration). Priests at St. Mary's noticed, in around 2009, exceedingly long lines for Confession on Good Friday. So they added more confession times, and have never stopped adding. Sociologists observe that Pentecostals have cut into Catholics' market dominance in Latin America with faith that is personal, warm, vibrant. Catholics have their own version of personal, warm, and vibrant, and it's working in these parishes. The Collingwood neighbourhood transitioned from largely white and middle class to everything else (pastoral assistant Vesna Jankovic estimates that their 10% non-Filipino population comes from 80 nationalities). Personality matters too. Priests in both settings have been well-liked. "These things go in cycles," Jankovic says. "We had a down cycle in the 70s. I attribute the change to John Paul II and Francis and their way with young people—they have moved a whole generation. Personality matters. Francis speaks well to my atheist relatives." The Catholics also have more theological diversity in their midst than any group I've looked at in the Lower Mainland. "We have both prolife and soup kitchen Catholics, social justice and cultural renewal people, peace activist nuns and fire-breathing bishop. And we have the numbers," Reid said. Catholic masses are full all over the city. The archdiocese can't open parishes fast enough.

Having taught for St. Mark's Roman Catholic College I have watched with curiosity as the Catholic presence in Vancouver has expanded these past several years. Under the wise leadership of Archbishop Michael Miller, the Roman Catholic Church has managed to broker good Gospel & culture connections in this so-called secular city. For example, in 2015 Archbishop Miller hosted a major event with Mayor Gregor Robinson (who arrived on his bicycle) for a conversation on faith and the environment (remember, the civil religion) in light of Pope Francis' timely Laudeto Si document on Christian responsibility for creation care. Mayor Robinson, who had previously had an audience with Pope Francis at the Vatican, said in an interview that he's never belonged to any organized religion but he is gratified to discover leading Christians are deeply engaged with scientists about climate change. "We have a common desire and intention to address the harm we have inflicted on the Earth. We have abused the gifts of God," said Miller, who oversees more than 400,000 Roman Catholics in Metro Vancouver and the Fraser Valley (Todd, 2015).

Clearly, God is on the move in Vancouver. Old faltering expressions of Christianity are fading, and the Triune God is raising up new witnessing communities in the midst of this post-Christendom City of Glass. Missional leadership today in this context takes seriously the need to help people take steps towards faith in Jesus through adult catechesis and conversion. In a post-Christendom world, no one is "born Christian" and so disciples are made with intention and long-term commitment on behalf of the mission community or congregation. Michael Frost (2011) states, "Missional Leaders don't see changing the church as central to their cause; they want to change the whole world" (p. 21). Participating in the Missio Dei that Frost (2011) calls, "the unstoppable program of God's unfurling kingdom on earth," Christian leaders cannot "even conceive of how to control it, package it, or franchise it" (p. 21). Freed from a Christendom past, Christian witness today in Vancouver is not trying to recover a time when the church had a privileged place in society. Instead, there is encouraging evidence of what a Christian minority looks like as "salt and light" in the community, pointing to the power and presence of the risen Christ at work in the world, in the midst of our ordinary, everyday lives.

At the end of one of those ordinary workdays, I waited for my bus home, mindful that the journey back through leafy green suburbs, the downtown core and up into the mountains of North Vancouver was really more a pilgrimage than a commute to be endured. Around me swirled a sea of humanity in multi-ethnic hues combined with an equally dazzling variety of beauty in God's creation. As a redeemed sinner and follower of the risen Christ, I looked around at this "City of Glass" through a doxological lens. I stepped off the bus in North Vancouver and thanked the bus driver, mindful of God's faithful presence all around me. I looked up at snow-capped mountains and gave God thanks for His ongoing redemptive mission in this fallen world. In the distance, the "City of Glass" shimmered in the setting sun and the scene before me felt charged by the presence of the Holy Spirit. The whole creation seemed to whisper the Creator's invitation to fallible, fragile creatures like you and me described in The Church of Scotland's Book of Common Order as "sent forth as your witnesses in the world, to tell others that, through wood and nails, you disempower our depravity and transform us by grace."

References

Reid, Angus. (2017, April). A Spectrum of Spirituality. Retrieved from http://angusreid.org/religion-in-canada-150/#part-2

Bauckham, Richard. (2003). Bible and Mission: Christian Witness in a Postmodern World. Grand Rapids: Baker.

Block, Tina. (2017). The Secular Northwest: Religion and Irreligion in Everyday Postwar Life. Vancouver: UBC Press.

Brent, Jang. (2017, January 3). Home Values Skyrocket in Vancouver. Retrieved from https://beta.theglobeandmail.com/real-estate/vancouver/home-values-skyrocket-in-vancouver-region/article33473392/

Byassee, Jason. (2016, October). "Cracks in Secularism: Thriving Churches in Vancouver." Christ and Cascadia Conference. Retrieved from https://theotherjournal.com/2017/06/07/cracks-secularism-thriving-churches-vancouver/

Coupland, Douglas. (2013). City of Glass. Vancouver: Douglas & McIntyre.

Frost, Michael. (2011). The Road to Missional: Journey to the Centre of the Church. Grand Rapids: Baker.

Hayward, Jonathan. (2017, January 23). Vancouver Housing Market Third most expensive in the world: survey. Globe and Mail. Retrieved from https://www.theglobeandmail.com/real-estate/vancouver/vancouvers-housing-market-third-most-expensive-in-the-world-survey/article33702895/

Jackson, Emily. (2015, April 16). Don't have 1 Million. Retrieved from http://www.metronews.ca/news/vancouver/2015/04/16/dont-have-1-million-vancouverites-twitter-campaign-draws-attention-to-unaffordable-city.html

Lockhart, Ross. (2016). Lessons from Laodicea: Missional Leadership in a Culture of Affluence. Eugene: Cascade. _____. (2016). Personal Interview with Jason Byassee.

Olivier, Cassidy. (2016, May 11). Student Owns $31.1-million Point Grey Mansion. Retrieved fromhttp://vancouversun.com/storyline/student-owns-31-1-million-point-grey-mansion

Rah, Soong-Chang. (2009). The Next Evangelicalism: Freeing the Church from Western Cultural Captivity. Downer's Grove: Intervarsity.

Schaefer, Douglas. (2016, December 15). Richmond churches push back against racist flyers by organizing rally. Retrieved from http://vancouversun.com/news/local-news/richmond-churches-push-back-at-racist-flyers-by-organizing-rally

Stats Can. (2011). City of Richmond. Retrieved from https://www.richmond.ca/ shared/assets/2006 Ethnicity20987. pdf

Sparks, Paul, Soeren, Tim & Friesen, Dwight. (Eds). (2014). The New Parish: How Neighborhood Churches are Transforming Mission, Discipleship and Community. Downers Grove: Intervarsity.

Todd, Douglas. (2014, March 28). Vancouver is the most 'Asian' city outside of Asia. Retrieved from http://vancouversun.com/life/vancouver-is-most-asian-city-outside-asia-what-are-the-ramifications

_____. (2015, October 23). The Climate is Changing. So is the Catholic Church. Accessed from http://vancouversun.com/news/staff-blogs/the-climate-is-changing-and-so-is-the-catholic-church

Truth and Reconciliation Commission. (2016). The Final Report. Retrieved fromhttp://nctr.ca/assets/reports/Final%20Reports/Volume_4_Missing_Children_English_Web.pdf

Vancouver, Census Profile. (2016). Retrieved from https://www12.statcan.gc.ca/census-recensement/2016/dp-pd/index-eng.cfm

Vancouver Foundation. (2012, June). Connections and Engagement. Retrieved fromhttps://www.vancouverfoundation.ca/sites/default/files/documents/VanFdn-SurveyResults-Report.pdf

Zussman, Richard. (2016, March 31). B.C. minimum wage now the lowest in Canada. Retrieved from http://www.cbc.ca/news/canada/british-columbia/bc-minimum-wage-lowest-canada-1.3515923

CHAPTER THREE

Kelowna, BC
Paul Martinson

The Sunny Okanagan: Unceded Territory of the Syilx.

I have a measure of ambivalence for the place I call home. The Soul of the City Project has been a rewarding incentive to proactively engage this very environment that has become the center of my family's life.

I have lived in the Okanagan Valley for over 25 years. Most of my ministry life has been focused in other locations traveling out from Kelowna and returning home. Since discernment regarding the soul of Kelowna has fueled this project, the whole endeavor triggered reflection on a personal as well as a city level. Part of that reflection has been a deepening appreciation for how I have been influenced by First Nation relationships. Therefore, it seemed only natural to draw upon our Canadian identity, what John Ralston Saul identifies as a subconscious "metisness", and a First Nations perspective indigenous to the Okanagan Valley, to help guide this discernment of Kelowna's city-soul. Both Saul and the Okanagan First Nations perspective are grounded in a secular humanist bias which dovetails well with Kelowna as a rather typical secular city in Canada, a decidedly secular nation. While there is a measure of appreciative inquiry in this approach, there is also a balance created that keeps me from becoming overly critical of the free-wheeling, secular urban soul of Kelowna.

***

After several decades of seeing a spiritual director, it seems that I am finally beginning to have insights about myself as a human being; soulful insights. I am amazed at the layered complexity of my own soul. Therefore, this challenge to write about the soul of a city seems to be a daunting task requiring soulfully-tuned curiosity, observation, discernment, and reflection. City "psychological evaluation" is not a hard science, nor something that easily submits to empirical study. Neither is city-soul insight exclusively a spiritual exercise that captures the heart of a city with a singular sweeping prophetic gaze or word. The writer of the Book of Hebrews might actually give a rough map for discernment in the phrase, "able to judge the thoughts and intents of the heart" (Heb 4:12b, NASB). What is perhaps true for individuals might also be true as people live together in the same place.

So, I will use the Hebrews grid and see if the thoughts and intents of Kelowna's soul (heart) might yield its character and personality through a discernment process. I will not be using an exclusively Biblical worldview in the discernment process. Places in and of themselves have a certain power to shape the beliefs of a city and its inhabitants. Belden Lane (1998) points us towards the integration of environment and spirituality in his book, *The Solace of Fierce Landscapes,* when he writes, "We have lost the ability even to heed the natural environment, much less to perceive it through the lens of a particular tradition. Modern western culture is largely shorn of attentiveness to both habitat and habitus. Where we live–– in what we are rooted–– no longer defines who we are. We have learned to distrust all disciplines of formative spiritual traditions, with their communal ways of perceiving the world. We have realized, in the end, the 'free individual' at the expense of a network of related meanings" (p. 12). While we have in general lost this way of knowing a particular place there are cultures where this skill-set has not entirely been lost.

Syilx (Okanagan) Territory

To expedite this study, I will use an indigenous community model borrowed from the Syilx (Okanagan) People. As occupiers of the Okanagan Valley ecosystem for at least the last couple of millennium they have something to contribute to the nature of the Okanagan Valley. Jeanette Armstrong, an Okanagan land-speaker, writes that the Syilx community is at its best when four voices are heard in deliberations surrounding community decisions. These four voices are the voice of the minority viewpoint, the voice of those that speak for the land, the voice of all the intertwined relationships, and the visionary voice of creative innovation. "All four of these components within a community can participate in a decision-making process. The process then becomes, in terms of a democratic process, a different one than Roberts Rules of Order. The process becomes something that is participatory, that is inclusive, and that gives people a deeper understanding of the variety of components that are required to create harmony within a community" (Armstrong, 2002. p. 3). While this model for community is rooted in indigenous history, there is enough contemporary humanism and secularity in the model to match Kelowna's soul as a secular city.[13] How might Kelowna's city-soul measure up to an indigenous culture model that has very deep roots in the stunning beauty of the Okanagan Valley?

Geography and History

Kelowna, British Columbia is the largest city in the Okanagan Valley, an ecosystem running north and south with Okanagan Lake dominating the valley floor framed by hills, benches, and ponderosa pines. Kelowna is a growing city (population 120,000+) midway along

---

[13] I am using secular in the sense that Charles Taylor defines "Secular." Taylor's notion of Secular is "an age of contested belief, where religious belief is no longer axiomatic. It's possible to imagine not believing in God," which opens the door for a society of "Exclusive Humanism, a worldview or social imaginary that is able to account for meaning and significance without any appeal to the divine or transcendence." (Smith, 2014. p .141).

the length of the Lake occupying the eastern bank spreading out along the natural contours of the Valley. This is a city of intentional suburbanization and urban sprawl interspersed with small-acreage orchards and vineyards. The car density per person is one of the highest for a city this size in Canada. Kelowna is not a walking city, rather one where an automobile is close to a necessity.

In most Canadian cities, history is a story of a vast uninhabited wilderness and some sort of founding father or group of founding settlers. For Kelowna it is Father Pandosy, a French Catholic Oblate priest, who was the first white settler in the Kelowna area in 1858. He set up a church and a school and attracted many settlers to the area. He founded the Okanagan Mission which was the first permanent white settlement in the British Columbia Interior aside from the forts of the Hudson Bay Company and the gold rush boomtowns of the Fraser Canyon.

Father Pandosy and the Okanagan Mission started what would eventually become the Kelowna story. But before their extensive experimentation in various agricultural ventures, the land was inhabited. The Syilx people lived on the same land as the early settlers. Their contact with white people was originally conditioned by their relationship with the fur-traders of the Northwest and Hudson Bay Companies. In fact, the hospitality of the Syilx was part of the success of the Hudson Bay Company (HBC) in Fort Kamloops (Armstrong, Derickson, Maracle, & Young-Ing, 1998. p.2). Principally, the HBC was a trading alliance between First Nations fur trappers, French speaking "voyageurs," Scottish tradesmen and British-owned trading posts. Long before the various colonies north of the United States of America joined together to become the Dominion of Canada, most of present-day Canada was "governed" by the Hudson Bay Company. Peter Newman (1987) in his trilogy of books on the Hudson Bay Company quotes Dr. W.

The Soul of the City

Kay Lamb, a fur trade historian: "The honoured old initials H B C have been interpreted facetiously as meaning 'Here Before Christ'; instead they might more fittingly be taken as signifying 'Here Before Canada.' And if this had not been so, it is likely that Canada as we know it today would not exist" (p. xxi).

The fur-trade business venture fostered the back-story of our Canadian identity that John Ralston Saul (2008) has identified as a complex Metis (mixed-blood) network of First Nations and European newcomers in familial-type alliances. This networked business worked well, as long as the fur trade remained viable. Once the Confederation of Canada was founded (1867), the relationships with indigenous peoples became more politicized and absorbed into the jurisdiction of the federal and provincial governments.

As the settlement of the Okanagan Valley increased, there was considerable pressure on the British Columbian government to establish reserves for First Nation peoples. This action would allow the settlers to formally own the lands they had settled. Native Reserves were established in the early 1900's around the same time Kelowna was incorporated. The Syilx opposed the whole process of establishing reserves without negotiated treaties. Hence, today while most of the reserves in BC are owned by First Nations, those same people call them "Unceded Territory," land not defined by bilateral treaty negotiations. The Syilx people living on the Kelowna side of Okanagan Lake were relocated to the western side of Lake Okanagan. During a period of attempting to negotiate treaties, an alliance of First Nation chiefs wrote a letter to Sir Wilfred Laurier, the Prime Minister of Canada. Hand-delivered to Laurier in Kamloops in 1910 the chiefs wrote warmly about their early relationships, as friendship with the "real whites" to differentiate them from the latter settlers. Here is an excerpt from the letter.

> We speak to you more freely because you are a member of the white race with whom we first became acquainted, and which we call in our tongue "real whites"....After the other whites came to this country in 1858 we differentiated them from the first whites as their manners were so much different, and we applied the term "real white" to the latter (viz., the fur-traders of the Northwest and HBC. As the majority of the companies' employees were French speaking, the term latterly became applied by us as a designation for the whole French race). The "real whites" we found to be good people. We could depend upon their word, and we trusted and respected them. They did not interfere with us or attempt to break up our tribal organizations, laws, and customs. They did not try to force their conceptions of things upon us to our harm. Nor did they stop us from catching fish, hunting, etc. They never tried to steal or appropriate our country, not take our food and life from us. They acknowledged our ownership of the country, and treated our chiefs as men. They were the first to find us in this country. We never asked them to come here, but nevertheless we treated them kindly and hospitably and helped them all we could. They had made themselves (as it were) our guests....As we found they did us no harm our friendship with them became lasting. . . The Chiefs of the Shuswap, Okanagan and Couteau or Thompson tribes – Per their secretary, J.A. Teit – (Saul, 2013. Kindle Location 2271-2284).

Sir Wilfred Laurier received the letter from the chiefs respectfully, but was not re-elected the following year. So the chiefs' plea for a fair and equitable treaty went largely unaddressed federally, remaining a British Columbian provincial matter. This was the era when residential schools were being established to solve the "Indian Problem" (sic) essentially defined as the non-integration of First Nations into the society of the newcomers/settlers in the land. The Okanagan children were uprooted from their families and sent to Kamloops or to the Kootenay's for residential education. The recent report from the Truth and Reconciliation Commission of Canada (2015) has well documented the "cultural genocide" that the colonization process in general and the residential schools in particular have had on multiple generations of First Nations families and communities. Ms. Armstrong (1990) writing about the Syilx peoples' first hand experiences with Canadian colonial forces states in unequivocal terms:

> There is no other word than totalitarianism which adequately describes the methods used to achieve the condition of my people today. Our people were not given choices. Our children, for generations, were seized from our communities and homes and placed in indoctrination camps until our language, our religion, our customs, our values and our social structures almost disappeared. This was the residential school experience. (Armstrong, 1990. p. 142).

Mark MacDonald, Indigenous Bishop of the Anglican Church of Canada, in a recent sermon mentioned passionately, "The colonialization actions of the Canadian Government and the Residential Schools system especially, have created a *deep moral wound* on the Canadian soul." He went on to say, "If this wound were healed all Canadians would benefit." (Macdonald, 2015). Having presented this quote to quite a few people in varying contexts the universal response has been one of respectful assent followed by a perplexed ambivalence regarding what to do next. Mark MacDonald's exhortation is itself an egalitarian, indigenous plea for Canadian social harmony. Balancing individual action and community welfare is rooted in an indigenous "society as an inclusive circle that can be enlarged. And if such an adaptation is handled right, all sides should be able to benefit" (Saul, 2008. p. 59).

Living Means Walking Together

Becoming rooted in a place is much more than being physically present in a locality. The soul needs to be engaged to the degree that belongingness becomes an experiential reality and neighborliness affects a bond with the other, whether the other is First Nation peoples, other ethnicities, other religions, or other cultures. It is ironic that the minority voice of the Syilx, is largely unheard in Kelowna, while, at the same time, their presence is regularly acknowledged. First Nation awareness is at an all-time high in schools from kindergarten to the university classroom, but it is the polite awareness that respectfully claps but goes no further. Perhaps, there are too many unhealed colonial issues. The over-arching shame exposed by the Truth and Reconciliation Commission highlights the paralysis of inaction.

A recent incident involving a high-profile rail-trail project reveals the very tension of a dominant city not hearing the heart of the minority First Nations' voice. The Canadian Pacific Rail Company recently sold the railroad right-of-way from Vernon to Kelowna which will become a walking, biking, hiking recreational trail along some very beautiful lake shore. This is a highly supported inter-community venture. The Okanagan Nation Alliance (representing 8 Syilx reserves) pointed out that a large portion of the trail will pass through the former Commonage Reserve, land given to the Syilx as reserve land, but expropriated in the 1870s. The Native dissent has been largely ignored, even though the First Nations themselves are generally positive about the project. I think all the Syilx people are really asking for is the common courtesy of historical recognition. Using the land recreationally for the good of all is good stewardship of the land and respects the First Nations history of the land.

National Identity and Local Identity

When the majority rules in Canadian politics, the fallout tends to violate the very story we tell ourselves about our own identity. The national myth articulates our Canadian self-identity as polite, tolerant, egalitarian, peace-loving, and consensus-preferential people. These qualities are accentuated in localized regions. Wendell Berry (1972) writes, "local life is intricately dependent, for its quality but also its continuance, upon local knowledge" (p. 65). But this "polite, tolerant, egalitarian, peace-loving, consensus preferential identity" is a threat to the First Nations people in the region. Jeanette Armstrong (2002) put it this way, "our Elders have said that unless we can 'Okanaganize' those people [the dominant, Western majority] in their thinking, we're all in danger in the Okanagan" (p. 7).

Meanwhile, many people with shallow roots in this part of Canada add diversity, but lack local insight into its history, ecology and relationships. Kelowna sports a recreational face with many retirees migrating from the colder parts of Canada to the sunny summers and milder winters of the Okanagan Valley. The recreational mindset tends to project a fun-loving, carefree exterior while urban social issues fester behind the image. In speaking to people in Kelowna, I have heard over and over that it is a beautiful place to live, but it has a "white-bread culture". This term seems to have a double meaning. White-bread is generic term meaning something that looks good, but without much substance, implying the same for the city. In addition there are the racial overtones of Caucasian dominance and minorities not particularly visible. Because most of minority issues are hidden, they rarely capture public attention.

Another local issue which has implications for the soul of Kelowna is jokingly referred to as the "Okanagan Sunshine Tax." This "tax" is the lower wages paid to workers in this city. Sunshine Tax logic moves along the lines that Kelowna is such a desirable recreational destination, that local employers are justified in paying lower wages. As a social issue the Sunshine Tax is one issue that reveals the pervasive duality between the rich and the poor. The rich get richer with paying out lower wages, and the poor get stuck in the working-poor syndrome. Changing this requires a sense of community beyond the scope of most Canadian cities, but not absent from First Nations communities.

John Ralston Saul has argued persuasively that Canadian identity is rooted in the alliances formed between First Nation peoples and the predominately French and British early settlers. In fact what Canadians currently call "multiculturalism" has it historical roots in First Nations hospitality to "others" (Saul, 2008). Those other peoples, our historical ancestors, were not perceived to be invading enemies, but potential trading partners and family members. Hence outsiders were included in the circle of First Nation relations. To achieve this inclusion of the other would require a non-monolithic culture based on continual negotiated relationships. Essentially, this is what most First Nations people consider the heart of community, "being in a circle of ongoing reconciliation capable of including the other" (Saul, 2008. p. 65). First Nations in general interpret reconciliation in a relational manner, not as a legalized requirement, nor an enforced legal policy. Reconciliation is friendship that exists in a dynamic negotiated manner.

Listening to the other, the minority voice, could become a distinguishing mark of Canadian identity, as well as, a community building block of the Syilx/Okanagan people. John Saul contends that the hybridized Canadian soul, identified as a cultural form of "Metisness", is in fact part of our national identity derived from our historical contact with First Nations. The process of harmonizing the minority requires negotiation, consensus decision-making, and common respect.

All of this could be summed up in the word "harmony" often used by First Nations people to describe the goal of community. Harmony is very close in definition to the Jewish concept of Shalom, an all-encompassing sense of peace and well-being in all domains of life. Randy Woodley (2010) captures the significance of the Harmony Way in the following quote:

> In their nature as constructs, shalom and the Native American Harmony Way have much in common. Shalom, like Harmony Way, is made up of numerous notions and values, with the whole being much greater than the sum of its parts. Both are meant to be a way of living life in concrete ways that include more than all the terms found within the construct. They both set forth practical steps included within a vision for living. They both require specific action when the harmony or shalom is broken. They both have justice, restoration, and continuous right living as their goal. And, perhaps most importantly, they both originate as the right path for living, being viewed as a gift from the Creator. (Kindle Edition, Location 70-74)

For a city to achieve this sort of harmony there seems to be an intentional visionary need to integrate the broader Canadian soul with the Okanagan Valley indigenous soul as a way forward. Kelowna's motto, "Fruitful in Unity," gives all sorts of latitude for this sort of harmony in relationships a place to flourish.

How Might the Christian Church Engage the Soul of This City?

One of institutions within the community that would naturally seem equipped to address the soul of a city would be the Christian Church. Kelowna has traditionally been described as part of the Canadian Bible Belt, but the overall cultural milieu of the city today is secular as is most of Canadian society. Canadian culture as a whole no longer places the Church in the center of a community, nor sees it as a pillar of social conscience. Nonetheless, Christian spirituality continues to invite the formation of community as an expression of Christian action. The Apostle Paul in his famous sermon on Mars Hill in Athens indicated that all people lived on the earth under God's authority:

> The God who made the world and all things in it, since He is Lord of heaven and earth, does not dwell in temples made with hands;...and he made from one , every nation of mankind to live on all the face of the earth, *having determined their appointed times, and the boundaries of their habitation*, that they should seek God, if perhaps they might grope for Him and find Him, though He is not far from each one of us; (Acts 17:24-27, NASB)

The scriptural perspective that Paul had as a Jewish/Christian missionary to Gentiles was a revelation from God that was to be integrated into the Gentiles' cultural background. How, as a Canadian city in the un-ceded territory of the Syilx people, might our national identity and our Okanagan Valley identity integrate this revelation locally? Randy Woodley (2001) highlights the native tribes of North America being gatekeepers over their traditional territory: "Each host people is a keeper or steward of their particular land. They are responsible to God for what occurs on the land He has entrusted to them" (p. 152). This adds a spiritual dimension to the land-speaker's voice.

One of the mistakes of the past was the introduction of a gospel wrapped in colonial coverings. With colonialism came the expectation of assimilation into another culture. The historical momentum of the early Church, however, was the very opposite. The gospel message was to be integrated into the listener's culture. Transformation, therefore, was to come from inside the culture, not as an outside imposition. In Kelowna, the only authentically land-based, indigenous cultural background is Syilx (Okanagan). Therefore, both our Canadian national identity and our Okanagan locality should influence us as an intuitive social conscience. This approaches a more holistic model that seeks harmony for the common good over against the cross-pressured individualism so prevalent in Western Society.

Canadians appreciate consensual forms of governance, yet this style of non-partisan dialogue takes more time and requires listening skills. Very practically, the Okanagan people are now a minority voice in their own historical territory. While they have a measure of self-government over their own reserves and a strong entrepreneurial drive to be successful, they have become the "other." How will we listen to them? One way to do so would be to listen to the Truth and Reconciliation Commission's recommendations. While there are 94 concrete recommendations, several are specifically addressed to faith organizations.[14] The purpose of the report was to expose many of the colonial injustices of the past, but to also point the way forward for an over-all healing through reconciliation. This is the very issue Mark MacDonald referred to as a "moral wound on the Canadian soul."

The Truth and Reconciliation document "Reconciliation" is used in a broad way to signify the fact that where injustice has been done there needs to be conscious recognition, followed by an apology, and a dismantling of structures that influenced those injustices. In a more grass roots definition most First Nations people that I have conversed with view reconciliation as a restoration of relationships based on negotiation, or, to put it another way, civil, respectful, and mutually satisfying relationships. If we could engage this very important current issue in Canada by going beyond the apology, to listening deeply to each other, it seems like it would help us hear many other voices that are

---

[14] Specifically Recommendations #48, 49, 58, 59, 60, and 61.

clamoring for attention. Listening to the minority voice is a place of learning that will require skills of dialogue that can be learned, but it takes time, patience and practice. In other words it requires continual relational transformation of all involved to be effective.

The voice of the land touches the nerve of most people. Climate-change, living green, being ecologically sensitive, living sustainably, eating and growing organically, and having a holistic lifestyle are part of the daily buzz of conversation. Yet the implications of listening to the land are very challenging to our whole Western, urban lifestyle. I was in Montreal twice this past winter. I envision Montreal as sitting heavy on the land with brick and stone buildings. Kelowna seems to sit more lightly on the land. Upon reflection though, the bricks, stone and density of Montreal are only in a different context. Kelowna too sits heavy on the land, but in a different way. Our city as a sprawled-out, suburbanizing development requires lots of water and lots of resources. We are creating a heavy environmental footprint of green lawns in a semi-arid climate. Too many people and too few basic resources limit growth and clashes with our archetype as a bustling center of recreation and summer fun.

I suspect listening to the land goes beyond most of these popular concerns to a much deeper and more intuitive sense of land, water, and environmental care. A hint that this deeper listening might be happening is the proposed restoration of the oxbows of the lower end of Kelowna's Mission Creek (Moore, 2015). The oxbows were straightened-out to create more farmland. To restore the meandering course of the creek is not just a nod to the past. Wise habitat management for spawning kokanee salmon, and recognition that the original straightening was an unwise tinkering with a sensitive ecosystem are good examples of riparian habitat restoration that is sensitive to multiple environmental factors. Another example is the xeriscaping of apple orchards in the Okanagan. Retaining the balance of population growth, agriculture, and the natural environment requires an environmental wisdom which integrates First Nations land speakers, concerned environmentalist, and perhaps even biblical activists.

It is a common occurrence in First Nations speeches for the speaker to end formally with the blessing, "All my relations." In a traditional way the speaker is holding his or her words before all their relations for approval, judgment, and critique. As long as this is not a cliché, "all my relations" is a powerful community building exercise since the speaker is not just sharing their own thoughts and ideas, but reflecting a community of people. One of the major challenges in all Western cultures including Kelowna, is the fragmentation of relationships ending in isolated and lonely individuals. The challenge in faith communities is to have authentic relationships with familial affection, not just relations based on common beliefs.

Let's take a moment before we conclude to look at the fourth voice of deliberation mentioned at the beginning of this chapter. The voice of the creative innovators in Syilx communities stands interconnected to the others in a deep way. The role of the innovators is to think outside the box and seek new creative ways to look at challenges. In Kelowna there are a wealth of innovators doing all sort of amazing things in diverse fields. Artists of music, dance, theater, spoken word, song; along with architects, ecologists, and gardeners, along with high-tech, computer animation, and gaming are all contributing to a highly creative innovative culture. Much of what is happening is more underground than in the limelight. Among Western creatives in general creative innovation is a solitary quest to be discovered and then taken into a community. However, it is innovators as servant leaders fully engaged in a community that seem most likely to navigate through the constant white waters of social and cultural change.

A reinvigoration of faith communities to engage with minorities, to respect the land, to nurture relations and to be creatively innovative would be positive contributions to the place we call home. Such a vision for community rings true in families, in cities, in ecosystems, and in nations. In addition one cannot sit by the sidelines and critique the surrounding culture of Kelowna, its very soul, without being willing to actively engage in some sort of participatory action. The Early Church actively engaged their environments with soulful purpose. Part of the theological motivation that fueled the actions of believers was a deeply held worldview that they were now Jesus' presence in the world in which they lived. Paradise was conceived as here and now, not as a future heaven detached from creation. Parker & Brock address that malady:

> The modern West has its own collective maladies and life-threatening addictions. The compulsions, stresses, and transpersonal forces that threaten people's lives cannot be addressed by individual willpower or personal lifestyle changes. Societies are collectively captive to disorders that endanger human life, the environment, and future generations. Climate change, patterns of overconsumption, and inequalities of wealth and poverty operate at complex social levels that require collective action to rectify. Facing the facts and recognizing what is wrong do not generate change without social movements and support systems . . . Paradise is not a private realm of personal spirituality—only communal practices and shared endeavors in ritually organized communities can open its gates. (Parker & Brock, 2009. Kindle location 2394-2400).

Paradise as God at work in the world through His people integrates Shalom and the Way of Harmony into the way life could be lived. One direct benefit of this soulful journey is a deep appreciation for where I live. I must be much more intentional about listening. Hearing the minority voice, listening to the land speakers, honoring the complexity of relationships, and inviting the innovators to engage creatively are all signposts to living more soulfully. There is likely a tipping point where enough participation may even heal a moral wound. Touching the soul of a city invites my involvement.

"Seek the welfare of the city where I have sent you into exile, and pray to the LORD on its behalf; for in its welfare you will have welfare" (Jeremiah 29:7, NASB).

References

Armstrong, Jeanette C. (1990). *The Disempowerment of First North American Native Peoples and Empowerment through their Writing.* Saskatchewan Writer's Guild 1990 Annual Conference. Penticton, BC: Theytus Books Ltd.

Armstrong, Jeanette C. (2002). *An Okanagan Worldview of Society.* Bioneers 2002 Conference.

Armstong, Derickson, Maracle & Young-Ing. (1998). *We Get Our Living like Milk from the Land.* Penticton, BC: Theytus Books Ltd.

Berry, Wendell. *A Continuous Harmony* (1972). Washington DC: Shoemaker Hoard Publishers.

Brown, Brene. *Daring Greatly* (2012). New York: Gotham Books. Kindle Edition.

Lane, Belden C. (1998). *The Solace of Fierce Landscapes.* New York: Oxford University Press.

Macdonald, M. (2015, June & July). *The Truth and Reconciliation Commissions Findings.* Speech presented in Sorrento Centre.

Moore, Wayne. (2015. Apr 13). Diverting Mission Creek. Retrieved from http://www.castanet.net/news/Kelowna/137485/Diverting-Mission-Creek

Newman, Peter C. (1987). *Caesars of the Wilderness.* Markham, Ontario: Penguin Books Canada Ltd.

Parker, Rebecca Ann & Brock, Rita Nakashima. (2009). *Saving Paradise: How Christianity Traded Love of this World for Crucifixion and Empire.* Boston: Beacon Press. Kindle Edition.

Saul, John Ralston. (2008). *A Fair Country.* Toronto: Penguin Books Canada Ltd.

Saul, John Ralston. (2014) *The Comeback: How Aboriginals are Reclaiming Power and Influence.* Toronto: Penguin Canada. Kindle Edition.

Smith, James K. A. (2014). *How (Not) to Be Secular: Reading Charles Taylor*. Grand Rapids: Wm. B. Eerdmans Publishing Co. Kindle Edition.

National Archives of Canada. *"The Indian Problem."* Record Group 10, vol. 6810, file 470-2-3, vol. 7, pp. 55 (L-3) and 63 (N-3). Retrieved from https://www.bac-lac.gc.ca/eng/discover/aboriginal-heritage/resources-researchers/Pages/residential-schools-resource-sheets.aspx

Truth and Reconciliation Commission of Canada (TRC, 2015), The Final Report. Retrieved from http://www.trc.ca/websites/trcinstitution/index.php?p=890.

Woodley, Randy. (2001). *Living in Color*. Grand Rapids: Chosen Books.

Woodley, Randy C. (2010). *Shalom and the Community of Creation: An Indigenous Vision.*. Grand Rapids: Eerdmans. Kindle Edition.

Hjalmarson

CHAPTER FOUR

Edmonton, Alberta: A FRONTIER CITY

Cory L. Seibel

A New Frontier for Our Family

My family and I relocated to Edmonton, Alberta, in the summer of 2013. This would prove to be a big move for us. Not only would we be making our home in Canada for the first time, but we had also chosen to move to North America's northernmost city. To reach this metropolitan population of over one million people, we would have to travel nearly 700 kilometers (435 miles) north from the US border. As we made this lengthy trip northward from Fresno, California, we wondered aloud about the new frontiers of experience that awaited us in our new home.

As we settled into this somewhat out-of-the way-destination, we discovered the immense beauty and cultural richness that Edmonton has to offer. The North Saskatchewan River valley, running through the heart of the city, comprises the longest continuous string of connected urban parkland in North America (City of Edmonton [COE], 2011b). Our family quickly grew to relish long bike rides along the trails that extend throughout Edmonton's "ribbon of green." We also discovered that, as "Canada's Festival City," Edmonton plays host to a dizzying array of celebrations over the course of a year. We came to appreciate the cherished place that the city's professional sports franchises hold within the hearts of its residents, for better or for worse. We became frequent patrons of a public library system that was recognized during our first year here with a prestigious international Library of the Year award. As my family and I delved into these varied facets of Edmonton life we found ourselves forging a deep connection to this city.

Exploring Edmonton as a Frontier City

Looking back now it is clear to me that Edmonton has opened wonderful new frontiers of experience for the members of our family. However, one does not have to look hard to recognize clues that the frontier experience is integral, not only to my family, but to Edmonton's character as a city. This is a *frontier city*. To help unpack this notion, I will draw briefly upon three definitions of the word "frontier" provided by *The Merriam-Webster Dictionary*. ("Frontier," Merriam-Webster, n.d.).

First, a frontier can be understood as "a region that forms the margin of settled or developed territory" ("Frontier," Merriam-Webster, n.d.). This definition certainly captures something of life in Edmonton. Alongside the beauty and refinement this city offers, there also is a discernible ruggedness to life here. This can be attributed in large measure to Edmonton's place as the gateway to the vast northern region of Alberta and the massive oil sands operations located there. Northern Alberta is by no means "undeveloped" in the strictest sense. However, as one travels to Edmonton's northern city limits, the expansiveness of the landscape leaves one with the distinct impression that this is indeed the frontier.

In distinction from Calgary, its "white collar" neighbour to the south, Edmonton's place within the Alberta economy entails a diverse workforce of "blue collar" trade specialists whose jobs support and sustain the oil and gas operations in the region. The local refineries and industrial complexes in which many workers labour, together with the countless oversized pickup trucks one encounters on the road each day, serve as continuous reminders that this is a city on the frontier. It has even been estimated that roughly 2,000 coyotes live within the city limits (together with innumerable jackrabbits), mostly in undeveloped areas of the river valley ("Coyote Sightings Spark Concern," 2015). Stated simply, alongside Edmonton's beauty and refinement, it is undoubtedly "rough around the edges." This is a frontier city.

Second, *The Merriam-Webster Dictionary* defines frontier as "a new field for exploitative or developmental activity" ("Frontier," Merriam-Webster, n.d.). This also helps to express something about the character of the city we now call home. This region has been inhabited by First Nations peoples for thousands of years, and European settlers have had an established presence here since 1795. This rich history is retold daily at Fort Edmonton Park, Canada's largest living history museum. As visitors there quickly discover, Edmonton is hardly a recent development.

Yet for all its history, Edmonton strikes me as an *emerging city*. In our time here, we have experienced this city as a vibrant place bustling with growth and development. This is attributable in part to Edmonton's robust economy. Even amid a significant slump in oil prices during 2014 and 2015, the diversity of Edmonton's economy has enabled the city to remain fairly optimistic and to continue on a growth trajectory. Because of Edmonton's reputation as a place of opportunity, significant numbers of people have relocated here from other provinces and countries in search of work. As a result, the population of Canada's fifth largest city grew by nearly 100,000 in five years' time, from 782,439 in 2009 to 877,926 in 2014 (COE, 2016). More recent census data released in 2017 revealed a population of 932,546 inhabitants and a growth rate that continues to outpace the national average for cities across Canada ("New Census Data," 2017).

Edmonton's optimism and relative prosperity is reflected in the widespread development occurring throughout the area. On the edges of the city, vast tracts of new neighbourhoods are being developed to keep pace with the demand for housing created by the growth in population. In the downtown corridor, several new high rise condo structures now stretch into the sky, with a handful more currently in the planning stages. Perhaps the most notable symbol of the city's growth and development is the Ice District currently under construction in downtown Edmonton. The centrepiece of this project is Rogers Place, the new, state of the art home of the Edmonton Oilers. Stantec Tower, another key piece of the Ice District plan, will hold the distinction of being the tallest building in Canada outside of Toronto upon its completion (Kent, 2015).

In the past, Edmontonians have suffered historically from perceptions of their city that are reflected in unflattering nicknames: "Deadmonton." Now, however, many residents have been emboldened with a confidence that this is a place where good things can happen, a place of possibility where creativity and ingenuity is welcome. This is attributable in part to youthful energy: with a median age in the mid-30s, energy and enthusiasm permeate the life of the city (COE, 2011a). However, factors like the historic developments occurring in Edmonton's downtown corridor also contribute to this optimistic ethos. This is reflected in the comments of Edmonton's thirty-something mayor, Don Iveson, regarding the boldness of the Stantec Tower project: "This is a massive gesture of confidence on the part of Edmontonians to have the audacity to build a building like this" (Clancy, 2016). In short, it is fair to say that the spirit in the air around Edmonton today is that of a frontier city as well.

A third definition offered by *Merriam-Webster* suggests that a frontier can be "a line of division between different or opposed things" ("Frontier," Merriam-Webster, n.d.). This definition carries immense significance in helping us understand Edmonton as a frontier city. When my family and I arrived here in the summer of 2013, we did so because I had been invited to join the pastoral team of Central Baptist Church. Thus, we were drawn to Edmonton with a keen sense that God was calling us to this place. Our expectation was not merely that this city would offer us new frontiers culturally, but that it would be a place in which we would experience new frontiers of God's Spirit at work. This would not be a matter of our "bringing" God's Spirit to Edmonton, but rather of our discerning and joining in what God was already doing in this place. We had left behind one urban context in order to make our home in a significantly different one. What would we discover?

After three years here, I still view the city through the eyes of a newcomer. This prevents me from describing Edmonton with the depth and nuance of one possessing a more longstanding history here. But I think it is fair to suggest that the fresh perspective I bring enables me to see things that long-term residents might miss. As I ponder what I have discovered thus far, I conclude that this city is a place where one encounters several important lines of "division between different or opposed things." Furthermore, I am convinced that these points of convergence provide crucial insight into the spiritual life of this city: they are the frontiers of God's activity here. I will devote the remainder of this chapter to exploring what I mean.

118 Avenue as a Frontier Point

One of the most important questions our family had to address in moving to Edmonton was determining where we would make our home within the city. Canada's high housing prices certainly helped simplify this decision for us. We concluded very quickly that we would not be able to afford to buy a house in many regions of the city. This led us to focus our search for a home within a cluster of mature neighbourhoods in northeast Edmonton where home prices seemed comparatively reasonable. Beyond the financial realities that influenced this search, we sensed that we were being drawn by God to make our home in this area of the city. Within a few weeks of our arrival in

Edmonton, we purchased a house just down the block from 118 Avenue and moved into our new neighbourhood soon thereafter.

In most communities, people's perceptions tend to be influenced by mental maps that overlay their city. For example, we might be accustomed to hearing about "bad neighbourhoods" or "the other side of the tracks." Our use of these descriptors reveals the invisible maps and boundaries that inform how we view the places we live. They reflect the significance that we assign to the various neighbourhoods that make up our communities. When one mentions areas like Old Strathcona, Oliver, or Millwoods, these names trigger certain associations among the city's residents. The meaning we attach to these locations reflects social perceptions of a neighbourhood's character, cultural makeup, or criminal elements. However, we also can assign spiritual significance to areas within the city. For example, some neighbourhoods gain reputations as being "dark" or even "God forsaken" places.

The avenue along which we chose to make our home is one of those places that bears a particular meaning in the minds of Edmontonians. When people from our church learned the location of our newly purchased house, their reactions ranged from alarm, to lauding us for having the courage to move into "that sort of neighbourhood." Historically, 118 Avenue has been viewed by many as a dark place within the city of Edmonton. The mention of this thoroughfare tends to conjure up sordid topics like drugs and prostitution. Over time, these sorts of social ills have plagued some of the neighbourhoods along the 118 Avenue corridor. However, this is hardly the whole story.

The mental maps adopted by the residents of any city are prone to be highly reductionistic in nature. They emphasize certain prominent characteristics while ignoring the nuance and the complexities. Perceptions of 118 Avenue reflect this tendency and obscure the reality. One can encounter many signs of vitality, culture, and beauty along 118

Avenue. For example, in traveling between 97 Street and 34 Street, one will come across restaurants and shops representing the cultures of more than sixteen different nations. Many Edmontonians have missed the diversity of people and places along 118 Avenue.

However, after three years here, it has become clear to me that 118 Avenue is a place where one will encounter many aspects of "convergence," the division between different or opposed things, to which I alluded above. This is one of the foremost locations in Edmonton where these convergences are manifest. Furthermore, contrary to how many Edmontonians view this area of the city, the frontiers one discovers along 118 Avenue do not exist in isolation from the broader context of Edmonton. Rather, they are acute manifestations of phenomena that occur across the life of the city. While this claim may surprise Edmontonians, the frontiers one encounters along 118 Avenue provide insight into the soul of the entire city. Moreover, these frontiers are signposts for the activity of the Spirit.

To unpack this assertion, I invite you to join me in taking a brief trip down 118 Avenue. In the remainder of this chapter we will visit three different neighbourhoods along this avenue. At each stop, I will introduce a significant frontier between different or opposing things to be found there, and explain how these convergences are reflective of broader dynamics within the Edmonton context. I also will endeavour to identify the frontiers of how God is at work in these places and, by extension, within the whole of the city. While hardly comprehensive, this should offer insight into the most significant frontiers of God's activity in Edmonton.

Beverly: A Frontier of Hope

Our trip begins at the end. The neighbourhood of Beverly is located on the edge of Edmonton at the easternmost border of 118

Avenue. Dating back to the late 1800s, Beverly was incorporated as an independent municipality in 1914. For many years, this town distinguished itself as a coal mining community with up to twenty mines in operation here. In the early 1960s, Beverly voted to become part of Edmonton when its expansion had reached the town's western border. Today, the Old Towne Beverly signs one encounters along 118 Avenue help to provoke a sense of nostalgia toward this unique heritage.

The neighbourhoods that once made up the town of Beverly are very different places today. Here in the streets along 118 Avenue, we find a striking convergence between the hopes carried by newcomers to Canada and the despair that plagues many of Edmonton's First Nations residents. The proportion of First Nations people in the Beverly Heights neighbourhood is more than two-and-a-half times larger than in the city at large (COE, "Beverly Heights," n.d.), while in the Abbottsfield neighbourhood it is more than three-and-a-half times larger (COE, "Abbottsfield," n.d.). In addition, there is a growing concentration of newcomers to Canada, including many immigrants from Congo, Rwanda, Burundi, Somalia, and a host of other countries. Many are refugees who have fled war torn regions of the world. The South Sudanese community has located its cultural centre in a storefront along 118 Avenue.

Both the First Nations and newcomer populations have been drawn to this area of the city by the concentration of affordable housing options. However, though the two populations coexist within this space, the trajectories that have brought them here are markedly different. The immigrants and refugees who make this neighbourhood home have come in search of a better future, for the stability and opportunity which were impossible in their countries of origin. Studies have shown that they have good reason to be optimistic. Canada has distinguished itself as a nation in which a high percentage of individuals can succeed at achieving upward social mobility (Lammam, Veldhuis, Palacios, & MacIntyre, 2016). Thus, for many of the immigrants who have begun their new life in Beverly's low income housing, this is not "the end of the line."

At the same time, according to one non-profit organization based in Beverly, many First Nations residents in this area of the city bear the marks of "the effects of multigenerational trauma as a result of residential schools, colonization, relocation, smallpox, inflicted Christianity, and loss of culture" (Red Road Healing Society, 2014). This multigenerational legacy continues to manifest itself in the lives of Beverly's First Nations population through "abuse, apathy, isolation, low self-esteem, stress, grief, addiction, violence and general pain" (Red Road Healing Society, 2014). For many of these people, this is a place where they find themselves "stuck" by a lack of options. Many residents carry the despair and marginalization common to First Nations people in Canada.

While the convergence between the experiences of immigrants and indigenous people is particularly visible in the stores and on the sidewalks of Beverly, it is not unique to this area. It reflects realities that can be found in a number of other corners of the city. According to data provided by Statistics Canada (2015), roughly one out of every five Edmontonians was born outside of Canada. While this percentage is not as high as Toronto, Montreal, or Vancouver, the aspirations associated with the immigrant experience have a far-reaching impact on the life of our city today. The frustration of their dreams has allowed some Somali young people to be drawn into gangs or into ISIS. However, the contribution of newcomers to Canada within this city is overwhelmingly one steeped in hope for the future.

The First Nations people's experience is also a significant dimension of the city's life as a whole. Among all Canadian metropolitan areas, only Winnipeg has a larger First Nations population than

Edmonton (Statistics Canada, 2010). It was with good reason that Edmonton was selected as the location of Canada's final Truth and Reconciliation Commission [TRC] gathering in March 2014. As the TRC (n.d.) has noted, "For 116 years, thousands of Aboriginal children in Alberta were sent to Indian Residential Schools funded by the federal government and run by the churches...There were more Indian Residential Schools in Alberta than in any other province." While not all First Nations people in this city are impacted by this legacy in the same way, the pain and struggle of Canada's indigenous people is felt widely here.

As I contemplate the frontier we encounter in Beverly and what it represents for the city at large, I am convinced that it raises questions about what it means for Edmonton to be a place where all people have opportunity to experience "a hope and a future" (Jeremiah 29:11). Clearly, this is a city in which large numbers of people enjoy prosperity and in which many have access to opportunity. But what exactly is the nature of the hope offered here? And who is it for, really? While the experience of Canada's newest residents gives rise to these questions, the experience of its original inhabitants does so to a greater extent. How might God wish to touch the most vulnerable and often-overlooked residents of Edmonton with a transformative hope?

Several local faith communities and other non-profit organizations in Beverly are striving to engage the residents of the community with a message of hope. Hope Mission's Tegler Youth Centre is perhaps the most prominent beacon here. From its facility on the corner of 118 Avenue and 38 Street, the Tegler Centre cultivates relationships with the children and youth of the neighbourhood, as well as their parents and other community members. Through Kids in Action, a free after-school program offered at several area schools, Tegler staff foster relationships with children and help them "learn their true potential" (Hope Mission, 2016). As they express it, "For a kid facing deep challenges, Kids in Action gives the most precious gift: the gift of hope" (Hope Mission, 2016). The faithful presence of the Tegler Centre is having a deeply positive impact in the lives of children and families in Beverly. Fortunately, there are organizations like this across the city, each of which is helping to transform the neighbourhoods of Edmonton as frontiers of hope.

Highlands: A Frontier of Community

As we depart Beverly and travel west along 118 Avenue, we cross 50 Street and reach the edge of the Highlands neighbourhood. If the neighbourhoods along 118 Avenue have a reputation for being plagued by poverty and crime, Highlands would be as a notable outlier. This neighbourhood was established around 1910 and developed gradually over a period of more than thirty years. Designed as a "streetcar suburb," Highlands has long enjoyed a strong sense of community (Alberta Community Development, 1993, p. 2). The historic character of this neighbourhood continues to be one of its greatest assets today. In 2012, *This Old House* magazine selected Highlands as one of the top ten "old house neighbourhoods" in Canada (Pandolfi, Shettleton, Barth, Martos, Santela, & Richards, 2012). The deep sense of community also continues to be one of this neighbourhood's distinguishing characteristics. Highlands has been described as a "little town in the city" (Haller, 2013), a place where people frequently meet up at the Mandolin coffeehouse, community garden, lawn bowling club, park, and curling rink.

In Highlands, we encounter the frontier between community and isolation. Despite a reputation for its strong sense of community, Highlands has not been exempt from the dynamics of relational isolation common in major cities today. While many are drawn to this neighbourhood by its historic charm, not everyone has moved here with an eagerness to connect with their neighbours. However, Highland's story has been strengthened profoundly by the Abundant Communities Initiative (ACI) undertaken here in recent years. ACI was begun by Howard Lawrence, a resident in Highlands who previously pastored a church in the neighbourhood. Howard's inspiration for birthing this initiative came from the vision of Asset-Based Community Development laid out in John McKnight and Peter Block's book, *The Abundant Community*.[15]

Launched under the auspices of the Highlands Community League, the ACI calls for Block Connectors to be recruited on each neighbourhood block. Each Block Connector would commit to engage his or her neighbours in intentional conversations around three themes: (1) what they like about and wish for their neighbourhood, (2) if there are specific activities in which they would like to engage with their neighbours (e.g., dog walking, book club, hockey, etc.), and (3) what talents and abilities they would be willing to contribute for the benefit of their neighbourhood. These ACI conversations have sparked a shared vision for the neighbourhood; new connections have been fostered between neighbours, and residents have become actively engaged in the life of their community. It has proven to be a powerful means of reversing relational isolation. As Anne Harvey, a key leader within this initiative, expresses, "The program makes neighbours out of strangers" (MacDonald, 2015).

During my first several years in Edmonton, I have been impressed by the city's high level of *social capital*, the social connections that exist among its residents. There are untold numbers of clubs, societies, and choirs in which one can become involved. A key vehicle of social capital resulted from a strategic decision made more than a

---

[15] John McKnight & Peter Block, *The Abundant Community: Awakening the Power of Families and Neighborhoods* (San Francisco: Berrett-Koehler Publishers, 2010).

century ago by a group of Edmonton's community leaders. They determined that each neighbourhood should have a community league. As a direct result there are 157 community leagues across the life of the city. These neighbourhood-level entities are connected under the umbrella of the Edmonton Federation of Community Leagues and are guided by a common mandate of "building better, stronger communities through inclusion, social action, by-partisanship, recreational and cultural development, and by providing the united voice of their community in the development of their neighbourhoods" (Edmonton Federation of Community Leagues, 2014). So, the value and importance of the neighbourhood has long been a part of the DNA of this city.

Given the positive results of ACI in Highlands, a number of community leagues across the city began to recognize the potential boost for their own mandate. As they acted on their interest, ACI has been implemented by more than two dozen community leagues in different corners of the city and now is known citywide as Abundant Community Edmonton (ACE). More recently, Lawrence has grown accustomed to receiving inquiries from leaders across North America, eager to learn how they can begin a similar initiative in their cities.

ACE is not a "faith-based" endeavour. However, in many neighbourhoods, people of faith have emerged as key leaders. In some cases local congregations have expressed a desire to be involved. ACE has connected deeply with the yearnings of people of faith to cultivate a spirituality rooted in place and to "seek the peace" of the communities in which they live (Jeremiah 29:7). ACE, says Lawrence (interview, August 6, 2016), has enabled "persons of peace" to exercise hospitality and pastoral care "on the block." It has promoted the purposes of God's reign at the neighbourhood level, he suggests, by encouraging "reconciliation and hope through the power of healthy relationships." This "rebooting" of neighbourhood-level social infrastructure is impacting the ethos and spirituality of neighbourhoods across Edmonton. In the process, it is leading to their transformation as frontiers of community.

Alberta Avenue: A Frontier of Justice

As we depart Highlands and travel west along 118 Avenue, we cross Wayne Gretzky Drive. Shortly thereafter we pass Northlands Coliseum, the storied former home of the Edmonton Oilers. Across the street lies the Northlands Expo complex, the location of the K-Days festival, held in late July each year and attracting 700,000-800,000 visitors. A few blocks down the road, after we have passed the Coliseum Light Rail Transit station, we enter the Alberta Avenue neighbourhood.

Many of Edmontonians' perceptions of 118 Avenue can be traced to the history of this neighbourhood. This history is recounted in a documentary entitled *The Avenue*, released in 2012.[16] As this film recounts, this locale began to take a downward turn in the early 1980s during a period of severe recession. Many people lost their homes and a number of local businesses closed. This decline in the area led to a high rental rate and contributed to the growth of "undesirable elements" in the area. By the late 2000s, this community was hounded by violence, drugs, and prostitution. In 2007, the Alberta Avenue neighbourhood received a quality of life rating of 0 out of 100. Community members were plagued by apathy, fear, and isolation. The area seemed to be a "zone of tolerance" for city leaders and law enforcement. Pretty much all media stories about the area were negative.

Finally, a group of residents decided that they had had enough. They began to engage in conversation about what they were experiencing in their neighbourhood. Two new community organizations were

---

[16] Unless otherwise noted, all historical information and quotes contained in this section are drawn from *The Avenue*.

birthed. The first, Community Response to Urban Disorder (CRUD) sought to deter crime in the area by sending groups out after dark to walk their dogs and engage in conversation with people they encountered along the way. A desire on the part of many residents to see their neighbourhood become a community arts district led to the formation of a second organization, Arts on the Ave. Soon thereafter, Arts on the Ave opened the Carrot Community Coffee House, which would serve as an important gathering place for the community.

As concerned citizens collaborated, they achieved some significant early victories for their neighbourhood. They became the first neighbourhood in Edmonton to win approval from the city to convert the local park, in this case an epicenter of drug and prostitution activity in the area, into an off-leash dog park. They also convinced the city to mandate the demolition of a hotel that had been a bastion of criminality in the area. A greater level of community and care started to develop among neighbours. There was a growing sense that a revolution was beginning to occur. "We Believe in 118" signs began to appear in storefront windows along the Avenue. People were encouraged to come out and participate, to try new things, and to see themselves as change-agents, able to make a difference in the community.

As community leaders engaged residents through surveys and community meetings, a shared vision for the neighbourhood emerged. Their priorities were expressed in a document entitled the *Avenue Initiative Revitalization*. They included making the Alberta Avenue area a safe community, somewhere that residents could have fun together, a good place to have a business, and a picturesque community with a "village" feel (Alberta Initiative Revitalization, n.d.). Under the leadership of Arts on the Ave, two new community festivals were launched. These brought neighbours together, attracted visitors from outside the area, and generated positive media coverage.

In a matter of a few short years, a great deal has happened in the Alberta Avenue area. Crime has decreased. The City of Edmonton now describes the revitalization effort here as the city's "pioneer neighbourhood revitalization project" (COE, "Beverly Heights," n.d.). In the face of this success, community leaders have realized that, if they are not careful, their neighbourhood could become a place where some residents end up experiencing exclusion. They have seen this occur elsewhere in the city and are determined to avoid repeating it. As Christy Morin, director of Arts on the Ave, expresses, "How do we change it and keep it affordable at the same time?" Morin adds that plans must be made to assure that people who live in the neighbourhood can continue to afford to live there fifteen years into the future. She and other community members do not want their neighborhood to fall victim to its own success.

The experience of the Alberta Avenue neighbourhood is a fascinating case study of the frontier between inclusion and exclusion. As its leaders recognize, when neighbourhoods become revitalized, home values tend to increase. As gentrification takes hold, the most vulnerable residents are at risk of being displaced. This is a significant issue in other areas of Edmonton today, most notably in the neighbourhoods immediately surrounding the downtown core. Around the time the new downtown hockey arena opened in September 2016, a number of newspaper stories were published chronicling the adverse impact that the changes in that area of the city were already having on residents living in affordable housing.

In addition, a few high-profile NIMBY ("not in my backyard") cases across the city in recent years have highlighted the fact that many residents are resistant to the idea of their neighbourhoods becoming places where socioeconomically inclusive community can occur. Even the Alberta Avenue neighbourhood has faced this struggle. In 2015,

Edmonton's development appeal board denied the Salvation Army's request to rebuild its Crossroads Community Church, located one block off of 118 Avenue, after neighbours voiced disapproval. Some saw the presence of the people served by the church as undermining the progress being made in revitalizing the community (Ross, 2015).

What does the future hold for Alberta Avenue and other neighbourhoods where the line of division between inclusion and exclusion is felt? As Bob Lupton (n.d.) reminds us, this question reveals something about the soul of a community. Lupton advocates for people of faith to play a role in advocating for "gentrification with justice." As he explains,

> Needed are gentry with vision who have compassionate hearts as well as real estate acumen. We need gentry whose understanding of community includes the less-advantaged, who will use their competencies and connections to ensure that their lower-income neighbors share a stake in their revitalizing neighborhood. The city needs land-owning residents who are also faith-motivated, who yield to the tenets of their faith in the inevitable tension between value of neighbor over value of property. (Lupton, 2007, p. 112.)

Fortunately, a number of Christian individuals and families who possess a deep commitment to seek justice in the way that Lupton describes have chosen to make their home in the Alberta Avenue neighbourhood. They are striving to help ensure that the forces of gentrification are not destructive to the life of their community and the vulnerable residents who live in it. We can only hope that, in other neighbourhoods impacted by the dynamics of gentrification, individuals will arise who can help them to become frontiers of justice.

Looking Forward to New Frontiers

An important truth about frontiers is that they are not static; they change with time. Some of the frontiers I have identified here would not have been as significant to the life of this city even ten years ago. Moving forward, additional frontiers will emerge. One need only travel a little farther down 118 Avenue to encounter a poignant illustration of this prospect.

A few blocks west of the Alberta Avenue neighbourhood, 118 Avenue dead-ends into the site of Blatchford, a neighbourhood that does not yet exist. Slated to be developed on the grounds of the now shuttered City Centre Airport, Blatchford has been envisioned by city officials as "a leader in environmentally-friendly community design," one that will "serve as a model for sustainable communities around the world" (Mertz, 2014). However, the cost associated with implementing this bold plan in its fullness has been the source of considerable controversy.

It will be interesting to watch how this situation continues to develop. What will happen in this new frontier where it seems that a line of division between economic interests and environmental stewardship is being drawn? In a very real sense, this site is representative of a tension that is native to the entire Edmonton region with its appetite for urban sprawl and its deeply entwined economic relationship with the oil industry. What will the Blatchford neighbourhood reveal about the soul of this community? How will this tension between fiscal pressures and the desire to care for Creation be resolved?

With time, we will have opportunity to reflect more fully upon this emerging frontier, as well as numerous others that we cannot even anticipate. If we remain open and attentive, we will surely continue to find that these lines of division constitute invitations to discover God at work. Indeed, we can be confident that, as we contemplate what God is doing in this place, Edmonton will never cease to be a frontier city.

References

Alberta *Edmonton Historical Walking and Driving Tours: The Highlands.* (1993). Edmonton: Alberta Community Development and the Highlands Historical Foundation.

Avenue Initiative Revitalization. (n.d.). About. Retrieved from http://www.avenueinitiative.ca/About.html

City of Edmonton. (2011a). *2011 National Population Census by Age and Gender.* Edmonton: City of Edmonton.

City of Edmonton. (2011b). River Valley. Retrieved from https://www.edmonton.ca/city_government/city_organization/river-valley.aspx

City of Edmonton. (2016). Detailed Census Results Comparison 2016 2014 2012 2009. Retrieved from https://www.edmonton.ca/city_government/documents/census/Detailed%20Census%20Results%20Comparison%202016%202014%202012%202009.pdf

City of Edmonton. (n.d.). *Neighbourhood Profiles: Abbottsfield.* Edmonton: City of Edmonton.

City of Edmonton. (n.d.). *Neighbourhood Profiles: Beverly Heights.* Edmonton: City of Edmonton.

Clancy, Clare. (2016, August 5). Tallest Building West of Toronto Reaches Construction Milestone for Edmonton's Stantec. *Edmonton Journal,* Retrieved from http://edmontonjournal.com/business/commercial-real-estate/grand-villa-casino-to-open-sept-7-in-the-ice-district

Clements, Jaimie. (Director). (2012). *The Avenue* [Motion Picture].

Coyote Sightings Spark Concern among Greenfield Residents. (2015, April 20). Retrieved from http://www.cbc.ca/news/canada/edmonton/coyote-sightings-spark-concern-among-greenfield-residents-1.3039934

Edmonton Federation of Community Leagues. (2014). History. Retrieved from http://efcl.org/about-us/history/

"Frontier." (n.d.). In *Merriam Webster Dictionary*, Retrieved from http://www.merriam-webster.com/dictionary/frontier

Haller, Cory. (2013, July). Little Town in the City: Highlands has a Small-Town Feel that Remains even as the Area Changes. *Avenue Edmonton*, Retrieved from http://www.avenueedmonton.com/July-2013/Little-Town-in-the-City/

Hope Mission. (2016). Kids and Youth. Retrieved from https://hopemission.com/kids-youth/

Kent, Gordon. (2015, September 16). Stantec Tower in Edmonton set to be Canada's tallest outside Toronto. *Edmonton Journal*, Retrieved from http://edmontonjournal.com/business/commercial-real-estate/stantec-tower-set-to-be-canadas-tallest-outside-toronto

Lammam, Charles, Veldhuis, Niels, Palacios, Milagros & MacIntyre, Hugh. (2016). *Measuring Income Mobility in Canada, 2016*. Calgary: Fraser Institute.

Lawrence, Howard. (2016, August 6). (C. Seibel, Interviewer).

Lupton, Robert. (n.d.). Gentrification with Justice. *By Faith Online*, Retrieved from http://sites.silaspartners.com/partner/Article_Display_Page/0,,PTID323422_CHID664014_CIID2235910,00.html

Lupton, Robert. (2007) Compassion, Justice and the Christian Life: Rethinking Ministry to the Poor. Ventura, CA: Regal Books

MacDonald, Alex. (2015, June 29). Making strangers into neighbours. Retrieved from https://transformingedmonton.ca/making-strangers-into-neighbours/

Mertz, Emily. (2014, December 3). Blatchford development recycling old airport hangars, runways. Retrieved from http://globalnews.ca/news/1706383/blatchford-development-recycling-old-airport-hangars-runways/

New census data: Edmonton-area population surges past national growth rate. (2017, February 9). Retrieved from http://www.cbc.ca/news/canada/edmonton/new-census-data-edmonton-area-population-surges-past-national-growth-rate-1.3971911

Pandolfi, Keith, Shettleton, Amanda, Barth, Gillian, Martos, Ambrose, Saatela, Elsa, & Richards, Meredith. (2012). Best Old House Neighborhoods 2012: Canada. Retrieved from https://www.thisoldhouse.com/ideas/best-old-house-neighborhoods-2012-canada

Ross, Andrea. (2015, April 10). Development board turns Salvation Army's request to rebuild Alberta Avenue church. *Edmonton Journal*, Retrieved from http://edmontonjournal.com/news/local-news/development-board-turns-salvation-armys-request-to-rebuild-alberta-avenue-church

Statistics Canada. (2010, February 26). 2006 Aboriginal Population Profile for Edmonton. Retrieved from http://www.statcan.gc.ca/pub/89-638-x/2010003/article/11077-eng.htm

Statistics Canada. (2015, November 27). Table 13.12 Foreign-born and visible minority populations, by census metropolitan area, 2006 and 2031. Retrieved from http://www.statcan.gc.ca/pub/11-402-x/2011000/chap/imm/tbl/tbl12-eng.htm

The Red Road Healing Society. (2014). Home. Retrieved from http://www.theredroad.ca/home.html

Truth and Reconciliation Commission of Canada. (n.d.). Alberta National Event. Retrieved from http://www.trc.ca/websites/alberta/index.php?p=766

Hjalmarson

CHAPTER FIVE

Calgary, Alberta
William McAlpine
Cow-town, Cultural Centre or Both?

"But seek the welfare of the city where I have sent you into exile, and pray to the Lord on its behalf, for in its welfare you will find your welfare." (Jeremiah 29:7)

The city of Calgary has been many things over the years – cow-town to cultural centre of Canada for the year 2012. Its citizens have ridden the wave of economic glory and apparent security, largely on the back of a vibrant energy sector. But they have also known the devastating tsunami of more than one economic downturn brought on by global recessions. Despite the rather checkered, ebb and flow of economic and political realities, Calgary is still home to, not only the headquarters of numerous key players within the corporate world, but also an impressive number of faith based or religious organizations.

Understanding Where We Have Come From: A Glance Backward:

Gaining an accurate understanding and appreciation of the current religious landscape of any city, and Calgary in particular is contingent upon an accurate grasp of where that city has been historically. Thus we begin this chapter with a very brief and woefully inadequate history of this wonderful city situated in the shadow of the Rocky Mountains. Founded at the junction of two rivers, The Bow and the Elbow, it was first named "The Bow" or "The Elbow Fort." For a very short time, it was named Brisebois by Inspector A.E. Brisebois of the North-West Mounted Police. This moniker proved unsatisfactory, however, to Brisebois' superior, Colonel James Macleod, who renamed the Fort Calgary after his home, Calgary Bay on the Isle of Mull in Scotland. The meaning of the word was thought by some to mean "clear running water," but more recently has been taken to mean "bay farm."

Under the North West Territories Ordinance, Calgary was incorporated as the town of Calgary on November 7, 1884 with a population of 506 people. Just under ten years later, on January 1, 1894, under chapter 33 of the North-West Territories Ordinance, Calgary was incorporated as the City of Calgary with a population that had grown to 3,900.

With consistent waves of migration from the East, Calgary reached a peak population of 47,000 by 1912. The discovery of oil in 1914 at what was known as the Dingman Well in Turner Valley just south of Calgary heralded a boom that was brought to a grinding halt with the onslaught of World War I. Thousands of young men left to support the war effort overseas; hundreds failed to return.

But by the mid 1920's Calgary picked up where it left off in 1914. It appeared this city would not look back – until the arrival of the Great Depression. The commencement of World War II in 1939 brought an end to the Depression and with it an enormous demand for oil and gas.

Like every other city in Canada, Calgary once again suffered the departure of thousands of young able-bodied men who went to join the war efforts overseas, many of whom would not return. But the post-war return to 'normality' and a trajectory toward prosperity was enhanced for Calgary with the discovery of an additional major oil supply a couple of hours north of the city in a place called Leduc.

The Soul of the City

By the 1950's Calgary became the fastest growing city in Canada, expanding from 100,000 in 1947 to 200,000 in 1955 and 325,000 by 1965. This trend continued for several years until at its peak up to 3000 new arrivals landed in the city per month. The surge caught City Councilors and City Planners completely off guard. There was no time to assemble a master plan and as a result much of the old Calgary was leveled in an almost panic-stricken effort to accommodate the influx. Building permits and approvals were dispensed with little or no thought being given to how any given structure would relate to or impinge upon the surrounding environs.

By 1982, however, Calgary found itself once again in the grip of a devastating recession. Hundreds of families were forced to walk away from the homes and mortgages. The vacancy rates among offices spaces in the city core soared from almost 0% to 20% and full employment sky-rocketed to 15% unemployment.

Yet despite such dark days of economic downturn there were one or two constants that remained throughout. One of those is an annual event that had its genesis prior to World War I – "The Greatest Outdoor Show on Earth." The Calgary Stampede has continued through boom and bust, when for 10 days every summer, business suits are exchanged for blue jeans, cowboy boots and Stetsons and over a million visitors celebrate the old Wild West that is an integral element of Calgary's history. A major piece of land has been dedicated for this annual party, situated in perhaps some of the most desirable and premier location in the city, now known as Stampede Park.

Despite the rhythm of economic bust and boom, the city of Calgary has continued to enjoy a fairly consistent rate of growth including seasons of unprecedented growth such as a record that was set between April of 2005 and April of 2006 when 35,681 people moved into the city, 25,794 of them coming from somewhere else. That means 71 people were moving into Calgary every day!

Calgary has proven itself to be a city whose spirit is not easily broken, having survived the loss of young lives during two World Wars and the devastating pulse of economic bust and boom. Without question, however, the one event in history that challenged the psychological, economical and personal heart and stamina of the city more than any other occurred on June 19, 2013 when after several days of unusually heavy rainfall, a flood occurred that was described by government officials as the worst in Alberta's history. 32 states of emergency were declared among communities along the banks and surrounding areas of the Bow, Elbow, Little Bow, Red Deer, Highwood and South Saskatchewan rivers. Total costs for damages were estimated at in excess of five billion dollars. Insurable losses mounted to the highest in Canadian history at approximately 1.7 billion dollars.

Within the city of Calgary 26 communities in the vicinity of the Elbow and Bow rivers were placed under mandatory evacuation orders affecting the displacement of over 75,000 people. The downtown core of the city, home to numerous major corporations and businesses and the approximately 350,000 people who work there, as well as several residential areas were rendered inaccessible for a week or more until the waters began to subside.

Two major landmarks among many suffered extensive damage: the Scotia Bank Saddledome in which the lower bowl of seating was covered in water up to the tenth row, and the Stampede grounds immediately adjacent to the Saddledome. All of this took place approximately two weeks prior to the opening of the annual Calgary Stampede exhibition and rodeo. The loss of revenue that would result from the cancellation of this annual event would have been nothing short of devastating to the city's economy.[17]

It was during this time of heart-wrenching natural disaster that the determination and timely action of a strong civic leadership that initiated effective emergency plans as well as an army of compassionate, sacrificial volunteers all rose to the top as it were, demonstrating that Calgary would once again, not only survive, but thrive.

It was during this time as well that countless volunteers under the direction of many faith based organizations stormed into action using social media, opening their homes to neighbours and strangers and providing the necessities of life to thousands of their fellow-citizens.

The Overall Lay of the Land

Before delving into the spiritual geography of Calgary, we would do well to have some understanding of the overall ethos and general makeup of the city. Calgary is divided into quadrants identified as the North West, North East, South East and South West. A report entitled "Calgary Snapshots 2015" authored by *Geodemographics, City Wide Policy and Integration Planning, Development & Assessment* provided some significant data on key elements of the various quadrants. For instance:

> 1) Calgary's boundaries include many features that influence development. The airport, for example, occupies a significant amount of land. While residential development is restricted on lands most affected by the operations of the airport and the noise of air traffic,

---

[17] It is worth noting that Calgary was but one of many smaller cities and towns that were devastated by this incredible force of nature, in particular High River, approximately 60 kilometers south of Calgary and numerous smaller communities to the west. It is estimated that High River will be rebuilding for the better part of a decade following the flood.

some types of industrial and commercial development are attracted to the

airport area.

- Fish Creek Provincial Park, described below also cuts a significant swath of land through the South West and South East quadrants on which no development, residential or commercial will occur for the long foreseeable future.

2) The centre sector or downtown core has 44% of the jobs in Calgary, but only 17% of the population. The south, west and northwest sectors combined have 46% of the population and 26% of the jobs.

3) For the past several years, City Planners, City Council, and, in particular, the city's current Mayor, Naheed Nemshi have made consistent efforts to attract more Calgarians to consider establishing their residences closer to or within the city core. The rationale behind this is that as the city expands wider and wider, costs incurred transportations systems and other infrastructure necessary to meets the needs of all citizens likewise escalate at an alarming rate. To date such efforts have enjoyed relatively little success. Land is at a premier or simply not available and rental costs are proving to be cost-prohibitive for the average income earner. As a result the vast majority of growth is occurring in the suburbs which is causing faith based organizations and Boards of Education to consider carefully their strategies for locating their various buildings.

Fish Creek Park: A Wilderness within Suburbia

One of the outstanding features of the city of Calgary that marks a commitment to the establishment and preservation of life-giving places within the confines of the city is a parkland that runs diagonally through the south east and south west quadrants known as Fish Creek Provincial Park. As noted above in the historical survey, such has not always been the case. Officially opened in 1975, this is one of the largest urban wildernesses in the world that provides just over 54 miles of excellent trails for cycling, hiking and/or jogging. Its footprint is three times the size of Stanley Park in Vancouver, British Columbia. Because the park is home to a number of bodies of water, including the Bow River, Sikome Aquatic Facility and the Glenmore Reservoir, to name a few, water sports and features are readily available as well including some of the best fly fishing venues in North America, if not the world.

Because of the rate at which Calgary has grown, the north, south and east boundaries of the park are now enclosed by urban sprawl which has spread well beyond the parameters of the park itself. On the west boundary the park is bordered by the territory belonging to the Tsuu T'ina Nation (Sarcee), a First Nation.

It is estimated that approximately 2.5 million people visit the park annually. Because of that, one of the on-going challenges facing city planners as well as Parks Canada is the protection of the wildlife and their habitat. The park has been established not only to preserve some of the wilderness in which Calgary was built, but to provide a place in which one may escape temporarily from the frenetic pace of urban existence in exchange for the serenity of a sanctuary within a natural setting.

Understanding the Religious Landscape of Calgary

There are several sources of data from which to glean a glimpse of the religious landscape of Calgary. These would include Statistics Canada, Canada Revenue Agency and the Calgary Foundation as well as a number of independent business and research groups such as Manta.com and Chimp.net.[18] Because lists generated by organizations such as CRA do not include entities representing a wider range of religious organizations beyond local congregations or places of worship,

---

[18] I am particularly indebted to the work of Milton Friesen and Cheryl Clieff and their excellent publication, *Strengthening Vital Signs Through Urban Religious Communities: Calgary City Soul*. (Cardus: 2014).

such as are included in lists assembled by Manta for instance, there is a significant variance in the number of identified faith based or religious organizations. For instance, in 2013 Manta identified 604 religious groups in Calgary while Chimp found 626, both of which were close to double the number identified by CRA for the same year.

Regardless of the number of faith based organizations and the protocol used to identify them, the data clearly indicates a strong presence of religious organizations in the city of Calgary, 55.6% of which are affiliated with Christian religions (Friessen and Clieff, 2014). Although only 12% of Calgary's population is self-identified with non-Christian religions, ethno-cultural diversity continues to increase. From 2006 to 2013, Calgary experienced an increase from 8% to 14% of people with non-Christian affiliation. Approximately half of this increase consisted of those representing the Muslim faith.

Distribution and Location of Faith Based Organizations

Christian churches appear to be relatively evenly distributed across the four quadrants of the city whereas other non-Christian religious groups appear to have areas of concentrated presence. The summary provided in the Calgary City Soul project demonstrates this as follows:

- Mosques are mostly represented in the NW and NE quadrants (eight organizations). There is only one organization located in the South, in the SW quadrant. All are located in a combination of urban and suburban locations.
- Jewish organizations follow a similar pattern as Mosques. There is a total of four organizations found, one in the NW, two in the NE and one in the SW. All Jewish organizations are in suburban communities as opposed to city centre/urban locations.

- Buddhist organizations are located in every quadrant except the NW. Under half (four) of the Buddhist organizations are located in or close to the inner city and the remainder in suburban areas (five).
- There is only one Hindu Temple, located in the NE
- There are four Sikh organizations, two located in the SW and two in the NE.

(Friessen and Clieff, 2014, p. 17)

It would appear that Calgary has shown itself to be one of the first Canadian major urban centres to take this whole matter of the role of faith based organizations seriously, to the point of affecting change in some of the city planning efforts. But other cities are also following suit (Daly, 2016.) This has not always been the case. It is only fairly recently that any kind of concerted effort has been invested in the determination of the role of religious communities and the kind of contributions they make to the delivery of social services and other urban issues. One of the most thorough and significant studies was conducted in 2009 by Cardus, "a think tank dedicated to the renewal of social architecture." This was fostered in large part to the fact that a report by the City of Calgary entitled *Centre City Plan* failed to identify faith based organizations as contributors to the establishment of a plan for community building. As a result of the efforts of the Cardus team and a number of subsequent sessions with City staff, a number of recommended amendments were approved by City Council on May 6, 2013 (Daly, 2016).

Because faith based organizations have been overlooked or not invited as conversation partners with City Planning departments, unintentionally or not, documentation on their contributions has been found to be rather thin and they input therefore misunderstood or not entirely appreciated. At the same time religious organizations have been challenged with the often daunting complexities of city planning processes.

The question that arises from this is, does the Calgary phenomenon stand as a one-off, unique situation or is it a common practice for civic authorities in other major cities across Canada to marginalize or exclude altogether religious organizations or faith institutions from the discussion table toward building a better urban experience and context?

Although interest in the impact of religious organizations or faith based institutions on urban planning has been less than robust to date, it has gained increased currency within the public arena through a variety of media and academic disciplines. For instance, in their efforts to measure the economic impact of religious organizations and in particular, local congregations, on communities, researchers at the University of Pennsylvania have coined the phrase the "halo effect." Lorna Dueck explained this phenomenon further when she stated:

> So what's the halo effect? It's a term coined by secular researchers at the University of Pennsylvania who questioned how to put a price tag on the investment that local congregations generate for the public good. They found that 12 Philadelphia congregations contributed $52-million in annual economic value to the city. More consumers put money directly into the economy, buying goods and services locally as weddings and funerals made the cash registers ring. Education and social services were part of the payoff, with programs for children, parents and the elderly. (Dueck, 2013)

If Canada were to have anything of semblance to a 'Bible belt' at least historically, it is fairly safe to say that Calgary finds itself located there. Should one question this suggestion, a brief survey of data

The Soul of the City

provided by Statistics Canada might encourage one to reconsider. A summary of the data generated by Statistics Canada census of 2001 and 2013 indicates the following:

Table 1: Religious Affiliations in Alberta, 2001 and 2011[19]

	Alberta (2001)	Alberta (2011)
Christian	2,099,435	2,152,200
Muslim	49,040	113,445
Jewish	11,085	10,900
Buddhist	33,410	44,410
Hindu	15,965	36,845
Sikh	23,470	52,335
Other religions	10,560	16,605
No religious affiliation	694,840	1,126,130

---

[19] Cited in Friesen, M. & Clieff, Cheryl. (2014). *Strengthening Vital Signs Through Urban Religious Communities: Calgary City Soul.* Cardus: Calgary, AB., 10.

As a result of the massive immigration shifts of the past decade in particular, Canada has become markedly more diverse. Calgary has also demonstrated very similar trends as those of Canada and Alberta.

Table 2: Religious Overview of Calgary, 2013[20]

Buddhist	23,260
Christian	667,110
Hindu	17,835
Jewish	6,170
Muslim	58,310
Sikh	30,420
Traditional/Aboriginal Spirituality	1,195
Other Religions	6,465
No Religious Affiliations	388,365

---

[20] Cited in Friesen, M. & Clieff, Cheryl. (2014). *Strengthening Vital Signs Through Urban Religious Communities: Calgary City Soul*. Cardus: Calgary, AB., 11.

Sacred Spaces in one of Canada's Most Multi-Cultural Cities.

It is not uncommon to find historically important buildings under the stewardship or ownership of faith based institutions. Calgary is home to a variety of such sites, a sampling of which is provided in a very insightful blog by Richelle Wiseman:

> In today's downtown Calgary, almost all of these historic buildings are home to congregations and a range of ministry activities and community services. They include St. Mary's Roman Catholic Cathedral (built in 1889), Central United Church (built in 1904 as Central Methodist Church), Church of the Redeemer (built in 1904), Grace Presbyterian Church (built in 1905), Trinity Lutheran Church (built in 1910), Knox United Church (originally Knox Presbyterian, built in 1912), Wesley Church (now the Calgary Opera Centre, built in 1911), and First Baptist (built in 1912). (Wiseman, 2011)

All of the buildings mentioned here remain standing to this day and feature prominently within the landscape of the city. Most have been designated as heritage or historic sites and therefore deemed places that merit that guardianship of regulations that prevent their removal or even major renovation. While for most, they continue to serve as home for local church congregations they also provide a place of remembrance and tradition, a concrete link to the past.

The fact that Calgary has emerged in recent years as one of the most multicultural cities in Canada should come as no surprise to anyone who takes a drive throughout the various parts of the city, and in particular the northeast quadrant. New residents who have ventured to Calgary literally from around the globe have brought with them their commitment to a wide array of cultural and religious practices and the concomitant need for sacred places in which those practices can be engaged.

It is significant to note the following:
- 25% of Calgary's residents are foreign born with over 120 languages spoken.
- In 2010 Calgary elected the first Muslim Mayor in Canada
- Calgary is home to the largest mosque in Canada, the Baitnunnur Mosque, at 48,000 square feet. (Battershill, 2011)

The multi-cultural dimension of the city has been redefined and protected by a number of pieces of legislation which are summarized in the following: Alberta primarily legislated the Alberta Cultural Heritage Act in 1984 and refined it with the Alberta Multiculturalism Act in 1990. The current legislation pertaining to multiculturalism is The Human Rights, Citizenship and Multiculturalism Act that passed in 1996. This current legislation deals with discrimination in race, religious beliefs, colour, gender, physical disability, age, marital status and sexual orientation, among other things. Alberta Human Rights chapter A25.5 states:

- multiculturalism describes the diverse racial and cultural composition of Alberta society and its importance is recognized in Alberta as a fundamental principle and a matter of public policy;
- it is recognized in Alberta as a fundamental principle and as a matter of public policy that all Albertans should share in an awareness and appreciation of the diverse racial and cultural composition of society and that the richness of life in Alberta is enhanced by sharing that diversity; and it is fitting that these principles be affirmed by the Legislature of Alberta in an enactment whereby

those equality rights and that diversity may be protected. (*The Human Rights, Citizenship and Multiculturalism Act*, 1996).

Planning Issues of Concern: Is There any Common Ground?

The challenges faced by Municipal Councilors and Planners in any town, village or city are complex and ever increasing. For example, how do we sustain a balance between providing space and infrastructure that will enhance the expansion of the community in the future and at the same time maintain critical links with the past? How do we attend to every citizen's needs through the provision of daily services while simultaneously exercising an ecologically astute sensitivity to the impact of such services on the environment?

Furthermore other realities must be factored into the urban equation such as the potentially enormous impact of numerous demographic shifts such as the ever-increasing numbers of Boomers who are stepping over the threshold into senior citizenship, and the steady stream of immigrants making their way into the city. Should concerns related to these realities be the private reserve of City Councilors and Planners? Should such things not also occupy the time, energy, and indeed, money of faith based organizations?

One could question the validity of investing effort into bridging the apparent gap between the various levels of city planning departments and faith based organizations on the basis of whether or not there is sufficient common ground. In other words, should religious or faith based organizations be concerned about and involved in the same issues as elected city officials and city planning departments? Well what are the issues? As a result of a citizen consultation at City Hall in February 2012, the City of Calgary identified the following planning concerns of particular importance:

- Parking and Zoning
- Developing and adapting suburban areas
- Social Service and volunteering
- Art, heritage and architecture
- Health and community safety
- Emergency Planning (Friesen & Clieff, 2014, p. 25)

An on-line survey conducted in 2013 under the direction of Cardus invited the participation of various religious organizations to determine if indeed there were any clearly identifiable shared concerns with those of city planners. Information gleaned from the survey indicated that participants identified social service and volunteering, developing and adapting suburban areas and health and community safety as the three most pressing issues. Despite the fact that not all religious groups are warm to the idea of participating in outreach or multi-faith work, plus the fact that not all faith based organizations "inherently see their role as caretakers of the broader community," (Friesen & Clieff, 2014, p. 25) there clearly is a role for such organizations particularly in the welcoming and assimilation of newcomers, providing support for cultural values and spiritual beliefs and practices.

If, as was demonstrated through the research efforts of Friesen and Clieff, there is significant common ground in which both city authorities and faith based organizations can and should be concerned, in what ways can and do religious organizations contribute to the welfare of the city of Calgary? What kinds of activities should they consider that may not be construed as primarily self-serving? In many instances major contributions are made through charities under the auspices of religious organizations of which Calgary has an impressive number. According to the 2013 CRA list of registered charities Calgary was home to 1022 charities.[21] One of the categories into which this list was divided[22] was identified as "Religion – Church and Other Places of Worship." Charities under this category represented 32% of the total number of charities within the city. Friesen and Clieff point out that "There were 161 Christian charities (49.8%), 11 Non-Christian charities (3.4%) and 151 charities not formally affiliated with a specific religion (46/8%)" (Friesen and Clieff, 2014, p.13).

The following table provided a complete list of all such charities and their sponsoring bodies:

Table 3: List of Registered Charities – Religion – Churches and Other Places of Worship[23]

CRA Code	Type of Religious Charity	Number of Charities
39	Other Denominations' Congregations or Parishes, (not else classified)	129
38	Roman Catholic Parishes and Chapels	25

---

[21] http//www.cra-arc.gc.ca/chrts-gvng/lstngs/menu-eng.html
The list included the following categories: welfare, health, education, religion, benefits to the community and others. (Friesen and Clieff, p. 13).
[23] http//www.cra-arc.gc.ca/chrts-gvng/lstngs/menu-eng.html

47	Missionary Organizations and Propagation of Gospel	25
31	Baptist Congregations	23
44	United Church Congregations	23
32	Lutheran Congregations	21
30	Anglican Parishes	20
49	Religious Organizations (not else classified)	18
37	Presbyterian Congregations	12
36	Pentecostal Congregations	7
35	Buddhist Religious Groups	6

34	Mennonite Congregations	5
43	(Religion) Charitable Organizations	4
60	Islamic Groups	3
48	Hindu Groups	2
33	Baha'i Religious Groups	0
40	Salvation Army Temples	0
41	Seventh Day Adventist Congregations	0
42	Synagogues	0
45	(Religion) Charitable Trusts	0
46	Convents and Monastaries	0

| 61 | Jehovah's Witnesses Congregations | 0 |
| 62 | Sikh Religious Groups | 0 |

When referring to religion in a community as expressed in planning reports at various levels, the language typically refers to the physical institution that is the building or facility. Exactly how significant that really is, is still up for debate. A report entitled "Imagine Calgary" was the only one of several similar reports that used the term 'all faiths.'

Conclusion:

To what degree is all of this information of interest to the broader religious community in the city of Calgary? Does it matter? Are we even aware? This has become a matter of interest and concern at several levels of political and social influence, even among the city fathers at City Hall. It seems that faith based organizations would be sadly remiss if we were to neglect or miss this window of opportunity to be a voice present at a number of tables of conversation. The fact that groups such as Cardus and individuals such as Lorna Dueck, columnist for the Globe and Mail and co-producer for the Television broadcast, *Context*, are doing the research and producing an increasing amount of helpful materials is most encouraging. But religious organizations must be intentional and wade into the present milieu in a manner characterized by grace and truth. For some this may require taking the risky venture out of their silo into the domain of public dialogue.

Toward the end of their excellent report, Milton Friesen and Cheryl Clieff provide some helpful observations and lessons which religious organizations in the city of Calgary would be wise to seriously consider. Included in these were the following:[24]

- The spectrum of faith based organizations in the city is wide and diverse in terms of size, focus, history, culture, goals etc. Such diversity comes with some significant challenges.
- It would appear that most faith based organizations are unaware of City Planning roles, timelines, processes and functions.
- There is no natural means whereby faith based organizations can learn about engaging strategically with the City outside the efforts of individuals on specific issues.
- Faith based organizations have no means of engaging with the City Planning as administrative peers.
- Faith based organizations have no central or consistent vehicle for communicating collectively with the City or with each other
- Faith based organizations are still in the possession of significant social capital such as volunteering, donating, and neighbourhood support.

At the opening convocation of Ambrose University in Calgary (September 8, 2016), President Gordon T. Smith admonished the University community with the words God gave His people through his prophet Jeremiah: "But seek the welfare of the city where I have sent you into exile, and pray to the Lord on its behalf, for in its welfare you will find your welfare." (Jer 29:7)

---

[24] See Friesen and Clieff, p. 41 for the complete list.

What would "seeking the welfare of Calgary" or any city for that matter, look like today? Embracing the separation of church and state must not be allowed to foster an isolationist posture wherein we as the church cloister ourselves in the safety of our silos. How will those who govern and plan for the future of our city know of our commitment to pray for and seek the welfare of our city if we are absent from the conversation table?

I recognize that this may be easier said than done due to the fact that not all government officials may be open or warm to the idea of having representatives from any religious organizations present. However, the example of Calgary as briefly addressed in this chapter hopefully demonstrates the fact that when the effort is made to reach out to such officials in a cooperative, grace-filled manner, significant results may well be on the horizon.

References:

Battershill, Cody. (2011, November). Calgary Cultural Capital of Canada. Retrieved from http://bestcalgaryhomes.com/calgary-cultural-capital-of-canada

Canada Revenue Agency (CRA). (2013). Charities Listing as of September 13, 2013. http//www.cra-arc.gc.ca/chrts-gvng/lstngs/menu-eng.html

Dueck, Lorna. (2013, April). Cities Should Give Thanks for Churches' Halo Effect. Retrieved from http://www.theglobeandmail.com/opinion/cities-should-give-thanks-for-churches-halo-effect/article10542051/

Daly, M.W. (2016, June). "The Halo Project Phase I: Valuing Toronto's Faith Congregations. Phase I Report of overall endeavor "The Halo Project." https://www.haloproject.ca/phase-1-toronto

Geodemographics, City Wide Policy and Integration Planning, Development & Assessment. (2015). "Calgary Snapshots."

The Human Rights, Citizenship and Multiculturalism Act . (1996). http://www.qp.alberta.ca/documents/Acts/A25P5.pdf

Friesen, M. & Clieff, Cheryl. (2014). *Strengthening Vital Signs Through Urban Religious Communities: Calgary City Soul*. Cardus: Calgary, AB.

Wiseman, R. (2011, June). Calgary's City Soul: A History of Religious Third Sector Activity. Retrieved from https://www.cardus.ca/policy/article/2816/blog/blog/blog/blog/

Hjalmarson

CHAPTER SIX

Regina, Saskatchewan
A Dialogue Between Spurgeon Root and Nick Helliwell

The Intersection of First Nations, Place, Immigration, and Globalization

I am a pastor at Healing Hearts Ministries in Regina, Saskatchewan. Healing Hearts is a 23 year old church plant in North Central Regina, a community known for addiction, violence, prostitution and gangs. *Maclean's Magazine* twice declared us the worst neighbourhood in Canada (Campbell, 2007; Gatehouse, 2007). That proclamation is now nine years old and debatable, but North Central remains one of the most notorious neighbourhoods in Canada. In the 17 years I've lived here with my wife and two daughters there have been 4 homicides, a police shooting, a death in a fire, a SWAT team raid, and numerous other less dramatic incidents within one block of our house.

It was not a theology of place, but the concept of Incarnation, that led my wife and I to move to this neighbourhood and raise our two daughters here (Perkins, 1995). "The Word became flesh and dwelt among us." I was working with youth, many of them First Nations, when we began the discussion of moving to this location. Once there, there was an almost immediate shift in our neighbours' attitudes when they realized we lived here. We were no longer outsiders, but people invested in the community who had also lost friends and neighbours to the voracious streets we called home.

In that journey I met my co-author, Nick Helliwell. I will let him offer his own introduction, but will say that he has been a close friend, brother and co-worker for over 15 years. He is the one I go to first when I'm lacking insight and experience around an issue facing First Nations (FN) people. His own journey as an aboriginal Christian has taught me a tremendous amount, and his theological insights and critique are as good as any I've encountered in seminary. The way we co-authored this paper was much the way our relationship works: I make some observations and then he offers his perspective. I want to avoid being another Muniow (white person) speaking for First Nations.

Let's start with the idea of place. Arguably, the problems in Regina are "people problems" not "location" or "place problems" and, in this sense, North Central is in no way unique. We may actually be a paradise compared to some urban environments where down-trodden minorities have gathered to try and make a living.

Nick: While I would certainly agree that the problems are "people problems," that is, that the problems and their solutions lie within people, I can see merit to the argument that location can greatly effect and determine what those problems are and their impact on various groups of people. Case in point: if you ask a non-First Nations person living in Regina where they are from (not their nationality), they will likely say Regina. If a FN person living in Regina asks another FN person living in Regina where they are from, they will name their 'home' reserve, even if they have never lived there.

Thus I am a First Nations pastor who has lived and worked in Regina all of my life, but I am from Peepeekisis – a small reserve about 100 km northeast of Regina. I have never lived there, but that is my home reserve – that is the band I belong to, that is where I am from. In a historically nomadic society, this would be important identification. Among post-Colonial Urban First Nations, your band is still a primary identity that says something of who you are. It is difficult for First Nations people to identify themselves with a place that is not connected to tribal heritage – connected to a people.

Spurgeon: I believe there are some unique factors to (the geography of) Saskatchewan and Regina and how it has been developed by the various colonizing powers. The city of Regina itself is a completely immigrant built space. Within the last few decades there have been nods in architecture to the First Nations who were here already, but Regina is an overwhelmingly Euro-Caucasian construct. Sadly, Regina is also rooted in the oppression and suppression of FN people. This was done overtly through Indian Residential Schools, forced Reserve placements and residency, and the repeated violation of Treaty 4.[25]

The Circle and the Square

In Treaty 4 territory, where Regina is located, the circle was, and still is, a foundational shape and structure in First Nations life. The Teepee, the round dance, the talking circle, and the symbol of the four directions are all circles. Life is a flowing cycle and there is an innate equality that comes when one is looking inwards at others in the community of a circle.

The colonizers who came to Saskatchewan, on the other hand, liked squares. There are now squares everywhere in the southern portion of the province: orderly, easy to survey, easy to map, easy to divide up and sell to other immigrants. In many rural parts of Saskatchewan "grid roads" are the staple navigational feature. Every two miles on the mile, following the grid, there is a road going north and south; then another road going east and west every one mile. This was the result of the

---

[25] Treaty 4 is a treaty established between Queen Victoria and the Cree and Saulteaux First Nation band governments. The area covered by Treaty 4 represents most of current day southern Saskatchewan, plus small portions of what are today western Manitoba and southeastern Alberta. This treaty is also called the "Qu'appelle Treaty," as its first signings were conducted at Fort Qu'Appelle, Saskatchewan on 15 September 1874. Additional signings or adhesions would continue until September 1877

Dominion Land Survey System, and while it was not implemented everywhere (geography interfered with the surveyors compass lines), vast swaths of flat prairie were divided up in this manner (ISC, n.d.).

Along with the roads came fences, telegraph lines, the railroad and eventually power lines, all running in orderly lines and grids across the (mostly) flat grasslands. One wonders what the First people thought when they came across these straight lines cutting across their home and circular world (McKay, 2009). This partitioning of creation for commercial purposes grew out of a weak reading of "subdue the earth" in Genesis 1:28, and without the counterpoint of Gen. 2:15.[26] Christian theology itself was colonized, with any Biblical passages implying power preferred over those passages that demanded servanthood, self-sacrifice, or care of others. This theology formed the built geography of our province and much of my city. The circle and the square are now a metaphor that describes the huge cultural difference between FN peoples and Euro-Caucasian settlers, and our attempt to force the circle into the square.

Nick: As our euro-western society becomes increasingly consumeristic, FN peoples are being changed dramatically as economics continues to dominate society. Women are advancing in almost every economic area of life as social and educational institutions, programs, as well as media messages all emphasize the role of women, and undermine the role of men. With incarceration rates of FN men being four times higher than FN women, women can get loans, travel, enroll in universities and land higher paying jobs more easily than men.

Which causes men to ask, "What is God doing? Does God care about me?" The church responds to inner city poverty most readily with programs for women and children. Kids camps, kids clubs, feed the

---

[26] The Lord God took the man and put him in the Garden of Eden to work it and take care of it.

children, women's bible studies, women's cooking, clubs etc. The men fall further and further behind. The church is not there for the men. It does not have answers for the FN men, and is not even asking, "What kind of help do First Nations men want or need?"

The church today does not understand FN men and it does not appear to be interested in them. The church appears from the perspective of FN men to be as racist and colonialist now as it was in 1880. In 1878 FN men in this land had a vital role in our societies for over a thousand years. In 1880 those roles were swept away. Our role as providers – gone. Our role as fathers – gone. Our role as protectors – gone. We have yet to recover our dignity. The Bible says we were created in God's image. That message is contrary to the message of the city, the church and our history. The plight of FN men is only one example of this. As illustrated by the juxtaposition of the Circle and the Square, the European reading of the Bible is contrary to a lot of things that First Nations people experience in the city of Regina.

Spurgeon: Even before the grids and squares came to dominate our province and city there were strong indications that First Nations and European views of place were at odds with one another. During the Treaty 4 negotiations Alexander Morris, the representative of the crown, and the chiefs who negotiated with him discussed the layouts of the camps where the two groups were staying. Morris had not set up camp with the First Nations, but was set off a little ways. The chiefs seemed concerned or perhaps confused as to why Morris and company were camped where they were. Morris explained about water, camp defense, and other pragmatic reasons for the camps placement and layout. The chiefs seemed mostly concerned about why the camps were not together. How could treaty be arrived at, and relationships built, when the two sides were not even camped together? The discussion circled around this for a while with neither side seeming able to clearly communicate their point or understand the other's perspective (Morris, 2012). Sadly, this state of affairs seems to have continued to the present day.

Nick: The communication problems are still there. Ask a non-First Nations person to read the Sermon on the Mount and say what it is about and you get a discussion on how Jesus changed the rules. Ask a FN person to do the same and you get a very different response. The Jewish people Jesus was speaking to were people with a strong oral tradition. The FN people understand this and take Matthew Ch 5, 6, and 7 as a whole; and thus hear a very different message. But Jesus was talking to people with a strong oral tradition. Matthew was able to hear that sermon once, and then to write it out years later accurately. FN people understand this – they have preserved songs, stories, histories, for generations in the same manner. I have seen men cry just from hearing the Sermon on the Mount in its entirety for the first time. Yet they were raised by the church and never heard the sermon in its entirety.

Spurgeon: The built space of the city of Regina displays the same proclivity for squares and grids but due to the fact that it is still a growing, adapting form there are interesting deviations and changes in developmental plans and construction. The modernist desire for order and to put things into boxes and convenient grids began to change after World War II. North Central, the downtown, Cathedral (for the most part) and other pre-World War II neighbourhoods are laid out in grid patterns. After World War II, neighbourhoods like Uplands, Englewood, and now Harbour Landing were built with sweeping cul-de-sacs, and other non-square arrangements (Mario, 2016). The decline of modernism and the rise of complexity began to impact how our city was constructed.

Nick: The change in the design of the neighborhoods is a concrete symbol of the barriers to full participation in modern society that FN people struggle with. The older neighborhoods are increasingly rental housing, thrift and discount stores, and storefront charitable organizations, pawn shops and repair shops. The southern half of the city with its malls, the Legislature, University, specialty shops and chic restaurants and winding drives and boulevards remains a different world and culture, out of reach for the inner city population.

A recent inner city rail yard redevelopment project proposal illustrates how blind the city is to this entrapment. All three proposed options call for 1200 living units to be built within 50 yards of the Main CN Rail line. Who would buy such a dwelling? What is nearby, but an avenue lined with bars? While providing welcome employment and new construction, I predict that it will quickly become a slum neighborhood, expanding the boundaries of the disenfranchised neighborhood that already exists.

Spurgeon: Interestingly, the end of the Modernist, grid line construction coincided with the termination of the Pass System under the Indian Act which stipulated that FN people needed permission from the Indian Agent to leave the reserve (Joseph, 2015). In 1951 the Pass System was revoked and thus began a slow influx of aboriginal people into Regina, not into the new neighbourhoods with curving streets, but the old grids of the old neighbourhoods. FN people went from being hemmed in on the reserve, and needing permission to leave, to being hemmed into the grids of North Central and blighted by urban poverty.

Nick: This migration into the inner city and what FN people encountered there was the incubation and genesis of the FN street gangs that have emerged over the past 25 years. It is a process which I personally experienced and witnessed. The inner city became a potpourri of First Nations cultures with few economic choices. It was literally immigration into a foreign culture. It was further driven by the fact that the First Nations WWII Veterans were not allowed to return to their home communities (Lerat, 2005). As with any other mass immigration movement, families sought out proximity to relatives and then pursued similar economic opportunities. Lacking any legitimate means of creating income, crime became a rational means of providing for one's family. Pursuing alliances with fledgling motorcycle gangs of the 50's and 60's crime families became *de rigueur* among urban FN people in the decades that followed. However, as migration increased and the demographics of inner city neighborhoods shifted, so did the alliance and loyalties of people involved in crime: from family relations to geographical locations - hence the incubation of street gangs.

This shift has and continues to have a devastating effect on propagation of FN culture, social structures and personal identity. FN urban populations are desperately trying to retain and regain a sense of identity as a people, but are fighting a losing battle. The message of the church throughout this era has overwhelmingly been that FN culture is evil; that in order to be saved from sin (i.e. from the trap of crime and poverty), you must relinquish your FN identity completely and become an imitation Euro-Caucasian, actively participating in the decimation and demise of your native culture.

Spurgeon: This conflict between the circle and the square gives physical expression to another difference between the settler populations and the original FN inhabitants. That difference is foundational to a discussion of theology of place. It reveals, ironically, that FN people in Saskatchewan and Regina have a very well developed and invested theology of place while those of us who have immigrated here, recently or in the more distant past, do not.

In *No Home Like Place*, Hjalmarson states that post-Enlightenment place has been traded for universalized "space." Moreover, place has been demoted in much Western theology, with heaven becoming the ultimate, other-worldly destination (Hjalmarson,

The Soul of the City

2015). As an immigrant population our ties to the land are naturally weak; we have all come from some place else. The Regina settlement is only 135 years old. Theology, necessity, economics: all of these impact large groups of people leaving one place and migrating to somewhere else. Not surprisingly, place in the new world became a backdrop to the drama, not very large in the imaginations of the settlers (Hopper, 2016).

Nick: An important distinction between the immigrant populations in Regina (all non-First Nations people) and the native population is that when a person immigrates from overseas, he leaves behind a homeland where he can be confident that his cultural heritage will be preserved. His language, indigenous customs, dress, ceremonies, etc. will survive and be passed on.

Not so with First Nations people, this *is* our homeland, and our culture is dying at an alarming and increasing rate. As discussed earlier, pressures created by the design and development or stagnation of inner city neighborhoods, limited economic opportunities and lack of understanding or encouragement of FN culture have all contributed to the demise of our heritage. Yet, for all that, and perhaps *because* of all that, Regina is an important location in First Nations history, culture and heritage.

The Regina plains played a significant role in the demise of the buffalo. The Cree called the place "oskana kâ-asastêki" (lit. *"Bones, which are piled")* the name in English, 'Pile O'Bones' being almost a joke among the European community for over a century, the annual fair being kicked off with a celebration on Pile O'Bones Sunday. Considered by FN people a patriot and hero, Louis Riel was brought to Regina to be hanged for treason after his troops were defeated by government forces in the North-West Rebellion in the spring of 1885. At the RCMP Training Depot the frame building built in 1885 which used to jail Indian prisoners who took part in that event (and the Duck Lake Uprising) is still standing. It was dedicated as a chapel in 1894 and still serves that function (Saskatchewan News Index, 2016).

The First Nations University in Regina is still fighting for national accreditation and autonomy, despite having been accredited and recognized by the United Nations.

The forerunner of the National Assembly of First Nations, the Federation of Saskatchewan Indian Nations, evolved from the pre-colonial political alliance on the Regina Plains between the Cree, Saulteaux, and Assiniboine peoples, known as the Iron Nation (FSIN, 2016). Although its predecessors organized as early as 1946, the Federation of Saskatchewan Indian Nations was not recognized by the Canadian nor Saskatchewan governments as a legitimate governing body until October, 1982. Most non-FN people are completely unaware of such racist policies, but more exist, too numerous to fully discuss here.

Spurgeon: For First Nations people, not just in Treaty 4 but in many locations and cultures around the world, place is vitally important and the land itself is seen as sacred. For many FN people this means they are spiritually connected to the earth they walk on. Picking up and moving isn't simply a matter of pragmatic economics; it would mean cutting the umbilical cord from the place that the Creator has placed you (McLeod, 2015).

Added to this, until the Reserve system was organized, FN were not just tied to the land, but to the buffalo, which were also irrevocably linked to the land. Buffalo provided everything that Treaty 4 First Nations needed and were a sacred provision of Mother Earth. While immigrants brought new economic systems with them, and brought jobs and new professions to North America, the Plains Indians lost their main resource, source of income and occupation. With the vanishing of the buffalo, the restriction of sacred connection to small parcels of prairie they couldn't leave, and the replacement of the circle with the square, the First Nation's social imaginary was deeply subverted.

In many ways the tension and problem around Treaty and keeping the numbered treaties can be seen as a conflict in a theology of place. From a government/immigrant perspective treaty is about access to resources, and like most contracts is exploited to its maximum and/or ignored until it is enforced. For a First Nations person, treaty is rooted in a sacred connection to a specific place. Recently this has led to interesting discussions and tensions as traditional teachings, ceremonies and protocols are reclaimed. These are *also* tied to a specific place, and for some First Nations it is vitally important that traditions from Treaty 4 are practiced in Regina and those traditions from other territories, say Treaty 6, are *not* to be practiced in Treaty 4 territory. So unlike most Western contracts or treaties, the numbered Treaties are very much seen as specific to a place, and non-applicable to other places.

So what does this all mean for my city and for someone who may be thinking of coming to Regina as an immigrant? First, while place may not be so important to an immigrant, it is integral to who FN people are and how they see themselves. This includes the political collision seen in the implementation and understanding of treaty and the built geography of Saskatchewan and Regina.

As a result, those hoping to have a positive impact on the First Nations community in Regina need to understand that we are not starting in a "neutral position" but one where Christianity has been the vehicle of oppression, colonization, and cultural genocide for over 100 years. While First Nations people tend to be very gracious and it would be rare for a Euro-Christian to hear it verbalized, we are the enemy. Anyone wanting to "do" Christianity with First Nations and in North Central Regina needs to understand this. It has greatly impacted my stance and approach in the community.

Nick: I was made aware of a recent gaff of evangelization when a well-meaning Christian friend of mine gave me a copy of a booklet he was handing out to local FN people as a means of communicating that FN people could be proud of their heritage. The booklet was entitled "Crow Heritage, and the Jesus Road." It featured a FN man in full regalia and featured stories of a number of Crow First Nations people who had come to know Jesus Christ as their savior around the end of the 19th century. If he had read the booklet, I doubt if my friend realized what the booklet communicated to the FN of Regina.

The Crow nation was one of the most feared and warring nations of the southern plains, being enemies of the Sioux, Cree and Assiniboine of the Regina Plains (McGinnis, 1990). The booklet featured as heroes several individuals who had fought on the side of Gen. Armstrong Custer against Sitting Bull at the Battle of Little Big Horn, and who were now buried at that National Memorial Cemetery with full military honors. The Crow people were responsible for Sitting Bull's exile into Canada and subsequent forced migration from Cypress hills in southwestern Saskatchewan to the Moose Mountains in the southeastern corner of the province. Two of the individuals featured in the booklet were directly responsible for Sitting Bull's surrender when they stole 100 horses from his band, thus depriving him of the means to continue his resistance to colonization. Many of the FN people my friend was trying to convince of the goodness of the gospel were descendants of Sitting Bull's band or of the friendly nations that tried to stand in support of him – including myself and my wife! The unintended message of my uninformed friend's efforts was that Jesus Christ helps those who help the colonization, demise and degradation of my ancestors.

Another example of offensive messages given by well-meaning believers is found in the gift of an altar to the Regina Prison Chapel. Donated by the Catholic Church some time ago, this 'impressive gift' was sanctified and dedicated by the church prior to installation. What makes the altar sacred, I am informed by a priest, is that under a small inlaid marble slab are, presumably, small fragments of the bones of a *bona fide* saint! As a First Nations person, I am deeply offended by the thought that the bones of a dead person are housed within the table top and that I am expected to treat this furnishing as the object that makes the chapel sacred space. This is found nowhere in scripture and violates my First Nations traditions and culture. What the church would call hagiolatry (worship or veneration of the saints) is to me necrolatry, or worship of the dead. Furthermore the Catholic Church that furnished the chapel ran the residential school that many of the inmates attended.

Conclusion

Spurgeon: In my opinion, the opening presentation of the Gospel in this community needs to be, "I will in no way oppress you or harm you. I want to understand who God has made you to be and help you become that person. May I join your circle?" Gutierrez (1988), the South American liberation theologian emphasized the need to "switch sides" for the Church and Christians, to stand against oppression rather than benefit from it and this is also the case in Regina and Canada as a whole.

After this one needs to be prepared for a lot of listening and a lot of "being in camp together." Morris negotiated the numbered treaties in separate camps and First Nations and immigrants have been in separate camps ever since, through the reserves originally (and still) stand now in the divide between inner-city neighbourhoods like North Central and the "nice" parts of the city. Most immigrants have never wanted to be in the same camp as First Nations but to simply gain what they can without true relationship. But without a covenantal perspective, this can only result in more colonization: the abstraction of space from place, and inevitable abuse. Committing to relationship, to community, to place, is vital to healing the chasm between First Nations, Christians, and the Church. This requires a "long obedience in the same direction" (Peterson, 2006) and means that solely programmatic approaches or "drive-by evangelism" is ineffective at best and likely harmful.

Finally I would strongly urge any believer to abandon any pretext or maintenance of power. The Church and Government of Canada misused Christian theology for hundreds of years to maintain power over First Nations people, and that is their sole experience of Christianity and the Church. This is a devastatingly sad irony to me since we claim to follow the one who gave up power and authority on an unprecedented level to save us (Philippians 2). The remedy to this is to seek to live out Jesus example of powerless servanthood to the disenfranchised.

Nick: Closely tied to a biblical reflection on Regina from the First Nations perspective is the need to resolve the conflict and perceived contradiction of cultural identity and Christianity. Both the FN and the Church need to seriously ask, "Is there an authentic Christian expression of First Nations heritage, identity and culture?" In Regina today, neither FN nor the Church have a satisfactory answer. The question that FN Christians need to identify, ask, explore and work toward resolution is; "How can I preserve and live out my cultural identity, language and heritage as a Christian?" First Nations people are asking the church, "Am I allowed to explore these questions without condemnation, disapproval or worse?" Will the Regina churches, as a 'people of Shalom' offer the First Nations people of Saskatchewan the help needed to find an authentic First Nations expression of their Christian faith?

References

Campbell, Colin. (2007, January 29). 'It's Not the Worst Neighbourhood'. *Macleans*. Retrieved from https://www.macleans.ca/archives/in-2007-canadas-worst neighbourhood-was-in-regina/

FSIN. (2016). FSIN History. Retrieved from http://www.sicc.sk.ca/archive/heritage/ethnography/fsin/fsi _history.html

Gatehouse, Johnathan. (2007, January 15). Canada's Worst Neighbourhood. *Macleans*. Retrieved from https://archive.macleans.ca/issue/20070115

Gutiérrez, Gustavo. (1988). *A Theology of Liberation: History, Politics, and Salvation*. Maryknoll, NY: Orbis Books.

Hjalmarson, Leonard. (2015). *No Home Like Place: A Christian Theology of Place* (2nd ed.). Portland, OR: Urban Loft Publishers.

Hopper, Tristin. (2016). Why Canadian White People Have So Much Trouble Understanding Why Somebody Wouldn't Want to Leave Attawapiskat. *National Post*. Retrieved April 28, 2016, from http://news.nationalpost.com/full-comment/tristin-hopper-why-canadian-white-people-have-so-much-trouble-understanding-why-somebody-wouldnt-want-to-leave-attawapiskat

ISC. (n.d.). Measuring Land in Saskatchewan. Retrieved from https://www.isc.ca/About/History/LandSurveys/MeasuringLa ndSask/Pages/default.aspx

Joseph, Bob. (2015). Indian Act and the Pass System. Retrieved from http://www.ictinc.ca/blog/indian-act-and-the-pass-system

Lerat, Harold. (2005). *Treaty Promises Indian Reality: Life on a Reserve*. Saskatoon: Purich Publishing.

Macdonald, Nancy. (2016, February 18). Canada's Prisons are the 'New Residential Schools'. *Macleans* Retrieved from https://www.macleans.ca/news/canada/canadas-prisons-are-the-new-residential-schools/

McGinnis, Anthony R. (1990). *Counting Coup and Cutting Horses: Intertibal Warfare on the Northern Plains 1738-1889*. Colorado: Cordillera Press.

McKay, Vincent. (2009). Chief Piapot: I Will Stop the Train. Calgary: Frontier Book Corporation.

McLeod, Toby. (2015). Indigenous Reflections on Christianity. Retrieved from http://blog.sacredland.org/indigenous-reflections-christianity

Morris, Alexander. (2012). *The Treaties of Canada with the Indians of Manitoba and the North-West Territories: Including the Negotiations on Which They Were Based, and Other Information Relating Thereto*. Lexington: Ulan Press.

Perkins, John. (1995). *Restoring At-risk Communities: Doing it Together*. Grand Rapids, MI: Baker Books.

Peterson, Eugene. (2006). A Long Obedience in the Same Direction: Discipleship in an Instant Society (20th Anniversary ed.): Downer's Grove: Intervarsity Press.

Saskatchewan News Index. (2016). Saskatchewan News Index: Top News Stories, Beginnings and Landmarks, RCMP Traditions Centre in Regina. Retrieved from http://library.usask.ca/sni/stories/beg24c.html

CHAPTER SEVEN

Winnipeg, Manitoba
Jamie Howison

"Ambivalence, Pride, and Prairie Island Pragmatism: Winnipeg's Spiritual Landscape"

> *I'm not sure what it is about Winnipeg that keeps me here, but I've lived here my entire life and it seems to me that it's my theme in a way, that I discovered happily about 20 years ago. It is sorta what I write about, it's what all my writing is filtered through; a kind of prism of Winnipeg. I'm still trying to get it right, I guess, so that's why I stay.*
> - John K. Samson

From time to time people ask me to speak on the story of saint benedict's table,[27] which is held out as a something of a success story in the Anglican Church of Canada. People want to know how we've grown and flourished over the years, from our first gathering of just nine people in May 2003 to a weekly average of a hundred and eighty in 2018. In an age when numbers are down, congregations aging, and many parishes face closure, amalgamation, and reduced clergy hours, here's this

---

[27] Saint benedict's table is a congregation of the Anglican Church of Canada, founded in 2004 as a worshipping community open to the cultivation of new expressions of music and art for the liturgy. While it shares church space with the Parish of All Saints' in Winnipeg, it functions as an entirely independent congregation of the Diocese of Rupert's Land, gathering for its Sunday liturgy in the evening.

Anglican congregation in Winnipeg that has apparently defied the odds. Sometimes people just want to hear a "good news" story, but I'm often aware some are looking for an answer, a strategy, a template. I've been invited to speak to various clergy and church groups from Halifax to Victoria, as well as at worship conferences hosted here in Winnipeg by the Canadian Mennonite University.

I always begin by saying that I could not parachute into some other city and launch a saint benedict's table 2.0, because what we have done is very much tied to our context, to Winnipeg. There are certainly some things that could be carried over to other contexts—that we have not been encumbered with owning a building, for instance, or that we gather in the evening rather than the morning—but I could hardly produce some "how-to" guide filled with bullet points and clever line drawings. Well, maybe I could, but it would eventually land in recycling boxes from Halifax to Victoria, just another spiral-bound resource that in the end simply could not deliver. No, there's something about Winnipeg that has made saint benedict's table what it is. So let me tell you about my city.

The weather. It is one thing that Winnipeggers can always make time to talk about. We follow the weather with at least as much enthusiasm as we do the Jets or the Bombers. We can be sure the winter will be long, the real questions being how deep the cold will go and how much snow will fall. We know that the three months of summer are likely to be hot, yet we watch the forecasts with a religious fervor, hoping beyond hope that the weekends will be clear and sunny for the lake, the park, the campground, the Winnipeg Folk Festival, or that outdoor wedding someone has risked planning. Spring and fall is when it all becomes unpredictable, as the temperatures fluctuate wildly between wintery and downright balmy. Last spring we hit a record high of 34.9 C on May 5, only to face snow flurries just a week later. Strangely, we are

The Soul of the City

always a little surprised when that sort of a slide happens, as if somehow this year's warm temperatures in early May meant the cold was done for the year.

It isn't naïveté that's at work but rather a resilient hopefulness of a sort that keeps us all here. We do know what we're up against with this climate, but we're determined to live in and through it all.

The filmmaker Guy Maddin, in his self-described "docu-fantasia" *My Winnipeg*, might have you think otherwise, but there is so much more to Winnipeg than a relentless winter. Frankly we tire of the nickname "Winter-peg," particularly when leveled against us by Torontonians or—worse—prairie people who have taken refuge on the West Coast. In Maddin's film, the narrator is desperate to escape a city of endless and soporific winter; a city in which he rides a seemingly destination-less train through snowy streets. "Winnipeg, Winnipeg. Snowy sleep-walking Winnipeg," the narrator comments as the film begins. "My home for my entire life. I need to get out of here. I must leave it now."[28]

That long winter does need to be embraced, otherwise it will beat you. We put the cold and snow of winter to work on our behalf in the same way that Judo teaches the student to use the opponent's weight and force against herself. Weekends find crowds flocking to The Forks to skate on the river and view the entries in the annual Warming Huts: An Art + Architecture Competition on Ice. Over two of the coldest weeks of the year people will climb down the river bank to dine at Raw: Almond, a gourmet restaurant set up in a large heated tent on the frozen river. For ten days in February people head to The Festival du Voyageur in Saint-Boniface to hear live music, wander through snow sculptures, ride ice slides, and dine on French Canadian pea soup and tourtiére.

---

[28] See the film trailer, http://www.imdb.com/title/tt1093842/

The arts scene thrives over the winter, as people venture out to unplug the block heater on their cars and head out for theatre, dance, opera, jazz, the symphony, the chamber orchestra, and choral music. The doors at venues like the West End Cultural Centre and the Park Theatre are put to heavy use through those months, with a steady offering of rock, hip hop, folk, roots, country, and blues offered up by both locals and touring artists. Sure, an occasional blizzard will get in the way, but even at -35° C you can still draw a pretty good house.

As soon as the summer arrives, we hit festival season in a big way. The Winnipeg Folk Festival is regarded as one of the best in the country, generally drawing a paid attendance of some 45,000 to Bird's Hill Provincial Park just north of the city. But there are also major jazz, fringe theatre, blues, and children's festivals, as well as an array of other outdoor summer events. The Old Market Square free stage in our historic Exchange district gets an awful lot of use during those warm months, the mosquitoes notwithstanding.

That's a lot of music and arts for a city of less than three quarters of a million residents, and there's even more when you include the amateur companies, dance and theatre schools, to say nothing at all of the people making music for the sheer love of it.

Since 2006 Winnipeg has been home to the annual festival *núna (now)*, described as an "Iceland Canada Art Convergence." Manitoba has the largest ethnic Icelandic population outside of Iceland, concentrated in Winnipeg and just north of the city on the shores of Lake Winnipeg. This festival is offered as a way of "maintaining the cultural bridge between the two places."[29] Yet what some of those artists have discovered along the way is an unexpected commonality between Iceland and Winnipeg, based in both being "island" cultures. Our ocean, of course, is prairie to the south and west, and lakes and forest to the north and east,

---

[29] More information on this festival is available at *http://nunanow.com/about-2/*

but we stand in the midst of it as a kind of island all the same. To reach the closest major city, one has to drive 750 km south to Minneapolis, 2000 km east to Toronto, or 1300 km west to Calgary. One might count Regina in that list, which is a mere 578 km west. However with a population of only 230,000—to say nothing of a football team with which we share a fierce rivalry—Winnipeggers are not inclined to count Saskatchewan's capital as a "major city."

What this means is that just as Iceland has developed a thriving arts scene that far exceeds what you might expect from a nation with a population of 330,000, so too has Winnipeg. Think of it as being a "if we don't do it, it won't happen" pragmatism. It is also a pragmatism that has sometimes allowed things to happen that some find surprisingly out of step with what might be expected of a mid-size prairie city. In 1998, Winnipeg elected Glen Murray as our mayor, the first openly gay mayor of any large North American city. This is something you would think might have happened in San Francisco or perhaps Vancouver. But Winnipeg? Yet what was clear was that Murray's sexual orientation was, at least for most voters, neither a reason to support nor oppose him. He was elected because he was seen as being the most creative and competent candidate for the job. Perhaps even more notable is the case of Communist Party of Canada member Joe Zuken, who in 1941 was elected to Winnipeg's school board, and then went on to serve as a city councilor for the city's North End from 1961 to 1983, distinguishing him as the longest serving elected Communist party politician on the continent. Notably Zuken won elections during the Cold War—against the background of the both the nuclear arms race and the Vietnam War. Yet, as was true in the case of Glen Murray's sexual orientation, Zuken was not elected because he was a communist, but rather on account of his reputation as a good and able advocate for his riding.

When it comes to our city, Winnipeggers can be fiercely proud, but somehow never prideful. Maybe that's the pragmatism at work again—we're just doing what needs to be done; no need to make a big fuss—but it is not only that. In *Stuck in the Middle: Dissenting Views of Winnipeg*, Bartley Kives calls Winnipeg "a city that inspires a profound sense of ambivalence among its residents."

> That has nothing to do with apathy, as there's no such thing as a Winnipegger without a strong opinion about the city. They either despise it or adore it, depending on the nanosecond and whether or not the bus came on time, the street happened to get plowed or the Blue Bombers won the previous night. While ambivalence of this sort is present in any city, only in Winnipeg does it serve as the defining character of the populace. (Scott & Kives, 2013, p. 6)

It is an ambivalence John K. Samson captures in "One Great City," a song written and recorded during his tenure with The Weakerthans. With its images of a dollar store clerk working in a lightless underground mall, a bus driver stuck in rush hour traffic and ruminating that "The Guess Who sucked, the Jets were lousy anyway," and the slow death of the North End, Samson's chorus is a simple "I hate Winnipeg." The words are placed on the lips of that store clerk and bus driver, but also in the "arcing wrecking ball" that swings over the North End, and in Weakerthans concerts no one sang out those words with more gusto than Winnipeggers. That includes Winnipeggers who have no intention of leaving the place, John K. Samson included.

In November 2015, as many of us lay in our beds listening to the morning news, we were delighted to hear that *National Geographic Traveler* had named our city "one of top 20 must-see places in the world."[30] How about that? We're right up there with New York City, Glasgow, and Bermuda. We let our hearts swell up with a bit of pride that day, many of us happily sharing the news on Facebook, hoping beyond hope that friends who'd left for Toronto or the West Coast would feel it as a little jab to the ribs. Yet underneath the pride of the morning there remained a very real level of disbelief. A top 20 must-see? Within a day the *Winnipeg Free Press* published a piece by journalist Randy Turner, which exemplifies that classic Winnipeg ambivalence to which Bartely Kives points. "Of course, Winnipeggers who fish-tailed to work on icy-roads Thursday and braced against winds gusting to 60 km/hr while trying to stay upright may have been the first to question *National Geographic*'s list. Winnipeg? Seriously?" (Turner, 2015).

Something of the same might be said regarding Maddin's *My Winnipeg*. We let our hearts swell with pride when the critical reviews began to flood in. The celebrity film critic Roger Ebert gave it four out of four stars, naming it the tenth best film of the decade. *My Winnipeg* landed on any number of critics' top ten lists of the best films of 2008, including those of Richard Corliss in *Time* magazine and of both Rick Groen and Liam Lacey in *The Globe and Mail*. Still, I wondered how many Winnipeggers had actually seen the film, and so I conducted an utterly unscientific social media poll. Of my Winnipeg-based Facebook friends I asked a simple question: "Have you ever seen Guy Maddin's film *My Winnipeg*?," adding that if anyone wanted to add any further comment they were certainly welcome to do so. Twenty-four hours later I'd received 115 replies, with 59 people indicating they'd seen the film, and 56 saying they hadn't. Frankly I was surprised that so many had seen it, though of course because my list of Facebook "friends" tends to be heavy on church people, university connections, artists and musicians, it

---

[30] The article is available at *http://travel.nationalgeographic.com/travel/best-trips-2016/#/bow-winnipeg-manitoba-hipsters_92381_600x450.jpg*

was anything but a representative sample of Winnipeggers. Those who chose to add comments tended to use words like "strange" and "quirky," with one person saying simply "baffled and intrigued." A former Winnipegger currently living in England noted that, "among a certain part of the cultured class over here, eyes light up when I tell them where I'm from, because they've seen the film!"

I was pleasantly surprised to see what amounted to a 50/50 split, as I honestly didn't think that even within my circles we had paid quite that much attention to Maddin's film. To my mind it does deserve attention, though it is likely true to say that the emphasis should be placed more on the title's "My" than on "Winnipeg." Winnipeg is not incidental, of course, but it is most definitely Guy Maddin's "Winnipeg" that the viewer bumps up against. For Winnipeggers viewing the film, things swung wildly between the familiar and the utterly strange, between fact and fancy. Oddly, though, even as Maddin had the train chugging through neighborhoods that have never seen a railroad track, he caught something that I found hard not to recognize. He tears into the city at so many levels, but in a way that is not entirely out of character for someone who has been raised here. Does he love the place? Does he grudgingly respect it, in all of its self-deprecating ambivalence? Does he see it as the only city that could have given rise to his strange cinematic visions? Probably all three, and more.

We have this pattern of *almost* hitting a home run, only to watch as the ball hits the top of the outfield fence and bounces back into the fielder's waiting glove. There's a lot of public green space in this city, but much of it is only marginally maintained. In 2003 the city opened Esplanade Riel, a landmark pedestrian bridge spanning the Red River and connecting the downtown to Saint-Boniface. The bridge incorporated a restaurant midway across the river, which was no small feat considering the need to supply both water and sewer lines. Much of the talk from city hall was how this would be a perfect location for a bistro specializing in Franco-Manitoban cuisine, yet the space's first tenant was a local burger and breakfast chain.

We've been talking about rapid transit for decades, to help make the long journey through our expansive city more manageable. In the 1950s it was a proposed subway system, in the 1960s a monorail line. Through the 1990s and early 2000s there was serious talk of a light rail transit line to connect the University of Manitoba to the city's downtown. In the end, we settled for a system of designated bus corridors, one short section of which is currently in service, with the proposed additions caught in a morass of controversy over land purchase prices and planned expropriations. At least one high profile city council member is actively working to quash the whole plan, leaving the system with just that one existing three-kilometer stretch.

More ominously, though, is that a city that is home to the Canadian Museum of Human Rights and hosts a very popular and successful two-week multicultural festival called Folklorama, was also named "Canada's most racist city" in a 2015 *Macleans* magazine article (Macdonald, 2015). Many of us bristled when we first heard of that designation, but it was hard to deny that we do have a deep, divisive problem. What that article had in view was not merely racism per se, but racism toward the city's Indigenous citizens. In response, Mayor Brian Bowman boldly declared 2016 the "Year of Reconciliation," which may or may not actually amount to anything lasting. Yet there does seem to be some fresh energy and resilient determination arising in both Indigenous and "settler" circles, so we might at least hope that this time the baseball will clear the outfield fence and we'll have something lasting to celebrate. Notably, just one year after that *Maclean's* article appeared, the magazine published a follow-up piece, "One year later: Winnipeg leaders on a city's fight against racism."

And here's the thing. We complain, we fret, we watch the near hits and misses, we bury our heads in the sand about some things, we even look askance at some of the very things about which we should be justly proud... and most of us stay. Roots and connections go deep here, and because it is still a mid-size city you're always liable to run into someone you know, particularly if your roots lie in one of the well-defined neighborhoods. What part of town did you grow up in? Where'd you go to high school? Did you ever go to see such-and-such a band when the Pyramid Cabaret was still the Spectrum? Are you any relation to so-and-so? She was my brother's first girlfriend! It is all commonplace kind of conversation here in a city often referred to as a "big small town." It does mean it can be a bit tough for newcomers to break in, of course; tough, but not impossible. Once you've made your way into one of those circles you'll find a real welcome, so long as you don't mind patiently waiting out the kinds of "connect the dots" pieces of conversation that Winnipeggers inevitably share. Besides, give it a couple of years, and you'll begin to be seen as one of the dots, however recently arrived.

But what does any of this have to do with the church and with the city's "spiritual geography?" A great deal, I would argue, because it is the kind of city where Maddin can make his film, where John K. Samson and the Weakerthans can sing out "I Hate Winnipeg," where a gay mayor and a communist city councilor can leave their marks, and where people will complain about the winter and yet line up to dine in a tent on the ice. It is a city whose streets are pocked with potholes from the heaving frost and ice, and in which we routinely say that we have only two seasons: winter and road construction. CAA Manitoba holds an annual campaign to name the worst roads in the province, and many Winnipeg drivers gleefully line up to see if they can't get their own street added to the list. While Scott & Kives (2013) suggest that, "Winnipeggers feel like they own the right to hate their own city (p. 64)," it might be more true to say that we reserve the right to name all that drives us crazy about a place we fear no one else in the country comes close to appreciating. It is a matter of pride again, though our self-deprecating complaining keeps us from arrogant pridefulness. So much is possible here.

While I believe that the story of saint benedict's table is very much connected to the city, we are hardly the only ones. I could direct you to the Little Flowers Community which thrives under the direction of author and pastor Jamie Arpin-Ricci, to the Winnipeg Vineyard Church, which is busily stretching the original Vineyard vision to incorporate both a more sacramental and liturgical sensibility and a vibrant ministry with and amongst the city's most marginalized, to the various "new monastic" and intentional communities that have sprung up in the city's core, to *The Meeting Place*, which has origins in the Willow Creek Church "seeker movement," but is now finding a way into a more robustly discipleship-based way of understanding its ministry. Jump back a generation or so, and I'd show you the birth of the Grain of Wheat Church Community, the inspiration for which came from Chicago's landmark evangelical activist church Reba Place. Keep rolling back through the decades and I could point to innovation after innovation, eventually landing on Elim Chapel, founded in 1910 by John Bellingham and my great-grandfather Sidney T. Smith as "place of refreshment" for people of all denominational stripes. Though a good part of Smith and Bellingham's project was to introduce this city to the dispensationalist theology generated in places like Dallas Theological Seminary and Moody Bible Institute, they also were driven by a concern for the bodies, hearts, and souls of the working class residents of their congregation's neighborhood. Given that Smith was also a highly successful grain merchant, his compassion for poor and working class people was hardly a foregone conclusion.

At precisely the same time that Bellingham and Smith were starting Elim Chapel, J.S. Woodsworth was serving as Superintendant of All People's Mission in the city's North End; an experience that would galvanize the young minister's commitment to socialist politics, leading ultimately to his role as one of founding figures in The Co-operative Commonwealth Federation (CCF), forerunner to the New Democratic Party. Woodsworth and Smith would find themselves on opposing sides during the 1919 Winnipeg General Strike, yet there is a real sense that the pragmatic "possibility" vision of each was very much tied to the ethos of the city in which their very different ministries were forged.

In the same way that Winnipeg simultaneously produced the grain baron Sidney Smith and the socialist J.S. Woodsworth, it continues to be a city in which such apparent contra-dictions continue to be played out. Right down the street from the Little Flowers Community, the Grain of Wheat Church continues to gather in an inner city church basement to explore and deepen its commitments to simplicity and service. Yet just ten kilometers away on the edge of the city sits Springs Church, a "prosperity Gospel" mega-church that draws thousands on any given weekend. Of Springs Church, the church historian Kate Bowler (2016) wrote that, "Growing up [in Winnipeg]... I had been taught in my Anabaptist Bible camp that there were few things closer to God's heart than pacifism, simplicity and the ability to compliment your neighbor's John Deere Turbo Combine without envy." She then continues,

> But when a number of Mennonites in my hometown began to give money to a pastor who drove a motorcycle onstage—a motorcycle they gave him for a new church holiday called "Pastor's Appreciation Day"—I was genuinely baffled. Everyone I interviewed was so sincere about wanting to gain wealth to bless others, too. But how could Mennonites, of all people—a tradition once suspicious of the shine of chrome bumpers and the

luxury of lace curtains—now attend a congregation with a love for unfettered accumulation? (Bowler, 2016)

Bowler's question is a good one, and maybe it can be partly answered by pointing to the city's longer story of being the sort of place that could produce both a Sidney Smith and a J.S. Woodworth. Somehow we make a strange sort of space for what seem to be utter contradictions, let things all sift and sort out over time, and on we go.

Bowler points to the presence of Mennonites in this city, and for anyone trying to understand the spiritual landscape of Winnipeg, the Mennonites cannot be ignored. Were I an English speaking Roman Catholic, I would need to talk about the presence of our city's large Filipino community: some 60,000, or close to 9% of the city's population. Were I located in the Roman Catholic Archdiocese of St Boniface, I would want to address the recent immigration of people from French-speaking African countries. Were I Ukrainian Catholic, I'd need to speak of the challenges of ministry in a context in which second, third, and fourth generation Ukrainian-Canadians have lost their language and feel an increasingly vestigial connection to their culture and roots. Were I a member of the Jewish community, I would be only too aware of the realities flagged by Allan Levine in a 2012 *Winnipeg Free Press* article :

> [A]s anti-Semitism diminished and opportunities opened, assimilation and inter-marriage have increased, and strict religious observance has declined. Winnipeg once boasted more than 20 synagogues and likely just as many kosher butcher shops; now it has half as many synagogues with dwindling membership, and no kosher butchers. (Levine, 2012)

Those are hard and challenging realities for a community that has made deep imprints on Winnipeg's social, political, economic, religious, and cultural life.

But I'm an Anglican, and so I need to talk about Mennonites.

Set aside the Roman Catholic and Orthodox churches, and you'll find that many of the truly flourishing church congregations in this city—regardless of denominational affiliation—will include some percentage of Mennonites. Though a high percentage is quite thoroughly acculturated in our city, there remains a fairly strong commitment to church attendance and a correspondingly strong commitment to financial giving. The education and faith-formation of young people is also highly valued, as is evidenced by the resources traditionally poured into private schools, church camps, and Bible colleges. Winnipeg's Canadian Mennonite University is a recent extension of this traditional value, and it is worth noting that a number of CMU students have opted to call saint benedict's table home during their time in Winnipeg.

In Andre Forget's (2016) online article outlining a proposed dialogue between the Anglican Church of Canada and the Mennonite Church Canada, Archdeacon Bruce Myers is quoted as saying that, "In Winnipeg especially…there are all sorts of people who happily migrate between [the Anglican churches of] St. Benedict's Table and St. Margaret's and Mennonite community churches, and are students at Canadian Mennonite University." Forget notes that, "Myers explained that many younger Mennonites have been drawn to Anglicanism because of its liturgical traditions and sense of 'sacramental life,'" to which I would add that it is not just "younger" Mennonites who are finding themselves drawn to the pews of those two congregations. And as I noted above, it isn't only these two that are benefitting from the presence of Mennonites, but also flourishing congregations of various traditions and denominations.

This may well be specific to this particular moment in time, as a good many Mennonite congregations of different conferences and affiliations are currently facing decline, and one of the city's Mennonite high schools is in something of an enrollment crisis. Another generation from now and many of the current commitments to church attendance, financial giving, and the education and faith-formation of young people may be even less visible, less pervasive.

But for now, in this moment, the presence of that population in Winnipeg is part of what has made for something of a perfect storm for saint benedict's table. Unlike so many people now in their 20s, 30s, and even 40s, if you grew up Mennonite you grew up church-connected. That church-connection is even stronger amongst those in their 50s, 60s, and 70s, and those age groups, too, are also well represented in our congregation. To be fair, Mennonites aren't the only ones who have brought such things to our community, for our numbers include people from Baptist, Salvationist, Pentecostal, Vineyard, and various non-denominational evangelical backgrounds, myself included. Yet the truth is that if all of our Mennonite members suddenly decided to leave, we would have a very hard time sustaining our life and ministry.

One other key characteristic of the Mennonite tradition that I need to highlight is its deep valuing of music, and particularly of congregational singing. In our context, this value dovetails with Winnipeg's strong music and arts scene, giving us a kind of embarrassment of riches when it comes to our own practice of music. Some twenty different musicians participate in one of our five regular music ensembles, with many of our leaders regularly writing new songs for use in our Sunday worship. We are unafraid to dig deep into more traditional hymnody as well, which combined with our own growing "canon" of original songs shapes and nurtures our community precisely by setting us loose to really sing. And sing we do, which is all part of the "perfect storm" we find ourselves riding.

Along with the city having a strong music and arts culture and a high percentage of Mennonites—and to be fair, a good number of those other church traditions I mentioned above—the other critical piece in our context is the sense of rootedness and connection that is so valued in this city. In our early years, most of the people who chose to engage with us as their worshipping community were either people to whom I was personally connected, or people connected to people with whom I had connections. I have often said that although we began to dream and envision what was to become saint benedict's table, about three years before we actually gathered for our first liturgy, unbeknownst to us things were actually being set in motion a good decade earlier, through the solidifying of a series of key friendships. The "dots" were very easily connected in those first few years, because everyone who came through the door tended to be arriving somewhat connected.

Finally, though, I believe that a big part of what made saint benedict's table happen, and a big part of what makes all of the other church and ministry innovations in this city possible, is found in what I called our "if we don't do it, it won't happen" prairie island pragmatism. This gives us some very strong willed people to work with—strong and creative, in fact, and actually not daunted by the prospect of failure. Give it a shot, regardless of what head office in Toronto is saying about slides in church attendance and affiliation. Nothing ventured, nothing gained.

Besides, the mercury in the thermometer is beginning to drop, and I hear there might be snow flurries tonight. Might as well dig in, and see what we can come up with to put on the community's collective plate for the coming winter.

References

Bowler, Kate. (2016, Feb. 13). Death, the Prosperity Gospel and Me. *The New York Times*. Retrieved from http://www.nytimes.com/2016/02/14/opinion/sunday/death-the-prosperity-gospel-and-me.html

Forget, André. (2016, April 2016). General Synod to Consider Bilateral Dialogue with Mennonites. Retrieved from http://cep.anglican.ca/general-synod-to-consider-bilateral-dialogue-with-mennonites/

Levine, Allan. (2012, May 26). The Jews of Manitoba, or 'The Centre of its Own Diaspora.' *Winnipeg Free Press*. Retrieved from http://www.winnipegfreepress.com/special/ourcityourworld/middle-east/the-jews-of-manitoba-or-the-centre-of-its-own-diaspora-154385665.html

Macdonald, Nancy. (2015, Jan. 22). Welcome to Winnipeg: Where Canada's Racism Problem is at its Worst. *Macleans*. Retrieved from http://www.macleans.ca/news/canada/welcome-to-winnipeg-where-canadas-racism-problem-is-at-its-worst/

Scott, Bryan, & Kives, Bartely (2013). *Stuck in the Middle: Dissenting Views of Winnipeg*. Winnipeg: Great Plains Publications.

Turner, Randy (2015, Nov. 19). Winnipeg Listed Among Top Destinations by National Geographic Traveler. *Winnipeg Free Press*. Retrieved from http://www.winnipegfreepress.com/local/Winnipeg-listed-among-top-destinations-by-National-Geographic-Traveler-351836841.htm

The Weakerthans. "One Great City." Reconstruction Site, 2003. John K. Samson.

Hjalmarson

CHAPTER EIGHT

Toronto, Ontario
James W. Watson

Toronto as a City Region

One of my introductions to the challenges of engaging the soul of Toronto came from a TTC[31] bus ride. I was riding from Pape subway station when a young man dressed in a lumberjack-style, plaid shirt and jeans stepped onto the crowded bus and said, "Hello everyone." He said it clearly and confidently and seemed genuinely cheerful.

The young man sat down and launched into conversation. "Why don't people talk to each other on the bus?" He asked his question very loudly on a very quiet bus. Our plaid neighbour had settled beside a very intelligent, articulate professional whom I had heard debate issues of religion and science (with some enthusiasm) when Mormon missionaries had once joined us on our bus. But this time I felt a bit sorry for him because it was clear he wasn't expecting to have a conversation partner that morning.

At the same time, I was fascinated. I do not know what was motivating the plaid guy, if he was conducting his own social experiment or if he wanted to do what he could to overcome isolation and loneliness in such a large city. The experience points to one of the realities of a large city: we encounter many strangers and we seem uncomfortable with them.

---

[31] Toronto Transit Commission.

My attempt to wrestle with the nature of Toronto outlines a couple of relevant themes that emerge from data and experience. I engage the Bible to provide an image intended to provoke personal prayerful reflection allowing us to consider what part we are being invited to play in God's unfolding, transformative story (*missio Dei*) of the city. Then I point to possible launch pads for engaging in spiritual discernment and action.

Biblical Perspectives and the Greater Golden Horseshoe Area

There are biblical examples of identifying and addressing the spirituality for particular cities. Jonah is sent by God to Nineveh and (eventually) addresses the problems God has identified. The people of Nineveh respond to the message, even if Jonah is perplexed by God's mercy. Jesus weeps over Jerusalem as the city which killed prophets and expresses desire to gather the people as a hen gathers her chicks (Matthew 23; Luke 13). Paul addresses the Areopagus in Athens regarding the religiosity of their city and uses the "idol to an unknown God" as a starting point for sharing about the nature and purpose of God (Acts 17). The use of different methods for identifying the nature of the city (spiritual discernment, prophetic insight, history, noting objects of devotion) and expressing the nature of the city in different ways (message, metaphor, concrete symbol) suggests that different options are available for us in describing the city. In considering Toronto as a gateway, mega-region we will explore one biblically grounded metaphor as a possible starting point for further theological reflection and action.

The Samaritan

Let us consider the role of the Samaritan[32] in Luke chapter 10 as a possible metaphor for relating to Toronto. We will consider the role

---

[32] Nowhere in the actual text is the Samaritan referred to as good, that is a title provided by editors (Thurén, 2014), however he is described as moved by pity and caring.

that the Samaritan plays within the story as an individual in transit who is of ambiguous ethnicity, questionable religiosity and compassionate intent as a possible metaphor for relating to strangers in the city. This perspective can provide a starting point for engaging questions of diversity and transition within neighbourhoods and networks. The central message of the parable is discussed by Jesus and the religious lawyer who is asked by Jesus, "Which of these three, do you think, was a neighbor to the man who fell into the hands of the robbers?" When he identifies, "The one who showed him mercy," Jesus said to him, "Go and do likewise" (verses 36-37). While the primary emphasis may be on the neighbourly activism of the Samaritan, there is also opportunity for reflection on his identity and role.

The Samaritan is chosen for this role based on his spiritual and cultural identity. While the priest and Levite may have been suspect in terms of piety to a Pharisee (Ringe, 1995) or religious lawyer, they would have had immediately identifiable religious and cultural identity. The identity of the Samaritan would have been questioned with regards to intentions and expectations of behaviour. Note that just a little earlier in Jesus' journey (Luke 9:53), the brothers James and John offered to call down fire on a Samaritan village (Parsons, 1995) which points to the animosity common towards Samaritans. The question of loving Samaritans or Gentiles in similar fashion to fellow Jews would have been well known (Thurén, 2014; Hendrickx, 1986). One proverb that depicts the tension states, "The one that eats the bread of the Samaritans is like to one what eats the flesh of swine" (Scott, 1990, p. 197). Fellowship with a Samaritan constituted a violation of a basic distinctive of the Jewish ethnic and faith community.

The conflict between traditional Jewish and Samaritan understanding of proper places of worship depicted in Jesus' dialogue with the woman at the well in the gospel of John (4:9) highlights the ongoing conflict. The Samaritans had a temple at Gerizim and their own "Samaritan Pentateuch" which was a particular redaction of the five books of Moses (Hultgren, 2000, p. 98). The conflict was both theological and a question of ancestry. The concerns extend back to the 8th century (722) B.C. conquest by the Assyrians (Hultgren, 2000; Ringe, 1995). While the Samaritans claimed to be descended from the Patriarchs, the Jews claimed they were heathen (Evans, 1990) as the King of Assyria imported people of other nations who worshipped foreign gods (Hultgren, 2000). Mixed ethnicity was assumed and spiritual commitments were suspect, with the Jews being suspicious of the Samaritans' relationships with the occupying and immigrant populations. In turn, the Samaritans were concerned about compromises the Jews may have made while in captivity (Ringe, 1995).

In this particular story, the Samaritan was also a traveler who had to stay in an inn, which could have indicated he was a "notoriously dishonest" trader or merchant as someone with "no social or economic claims on anyone's hospitality" (Ringe, 1995, p. 158). He was not rooted in a particular community close to the Jericho road. We do not want to stretch the analysis of this particular character too far, but these inferences contribute to building a profile. To the listeners of this parable the simple identification of this character as Samaritan raised doubts, or assumptions, regarding the cultural, theological and ethical convictions of this man who is travelling through the scene. The description of his actions in offering care to a fellow injured traveler subverts prejudice and raises interest among contemporary readers of the parable in Jesus' definition of neighborliness.

A City of Diversity and Transition

Could the image of the Samaritan serve as an image for the soul of Toronto? This particular character provides a metaphor that reflects the themes of diversity and transition, but also points toward constructive interaction. These two concepts can summarize a substantial range of Toronto's contemporary experience. The terms diversity and transition are selected both to address dominant themes currently influential in the experience of the city region and also to be neither overly positive nor overly negative. We can identify challenges in either diversity or transition but both provide opportunities if we have our eyes and ears open to the people around us. The extent to which these themes affect the lives of residents, workers and commuters will be determined by how they play out within specific neighbourhoods and networks of relationships.

Diversity

With the breadth of different immigrants who are arriving (Hiebert, 2015), along with multi-generational Canadians of a variety of heritages and First Nations people,[33] diversity is an obvious key word.[34] Toronto is renowned as a global, gateway city (Lo, 2008). Recent annual proportions of immigrants locating to Toronto are double that of the next two most attractive of the big three immigrant receiving centres in Canada (Vancouver and Montreal) and over half of residents are projected to have been born in another country by 2036 (Simmons & Bourne, 2013). One interesting project has involved a photographer and his team attempting to provide portraits of Torontonians who were born in different countries, however it has expanded to include Canadian born

---

[33] According to the 2011 census there were 36,995 Aboriginal people living in Toronto with off-reserve Aboriginals being the fastest growing segment of the Canadian population (Indigenous and Northern Affairs Canada, 2016).

[34] Wherever possible, references have been drawn from social inquiry, practical theology and missiological sources which are specific to Canada. While there are many valuable contributions to understanding the issues engaging Toronto from parts of the world affected by similar trends (such as urbanization and globalization), the limiting of references has been intentional to highlight Canadian (and wherever possible, Torontonian) material. The sources here reflect both secular and Christian (particularly evangelical) perspectives.

people as well (Shafer, 2014). The variety of backgrounds is only overshadowed by the diversity of life stories shared in the brief captions.

Migrants contribute to the religious diversity. From a review of 2010 migration, 59% of immigrants to Canada identified as Christian, 24% other religions and 17% unaffiliated, compared to 25% of non-immigrants indicating no religious affiliation and 3% identifying with religions other than Christianity (Connor, 2014). Christians coming to Canada are connecting to established, international, denominational traditions such as Roman Catholicism (Bibby, 2012) and Pentecostalism (Wilkinson, 2006) or are starting their own congregations (or movements). Some are intentionally sent as missionaries.

Dr. Narry F. Santos was commissioned from Greenhills Christian Fellowship (GCF) in Manila, Philippines to follow the migration path of families from their church to Toronto. With a vision of missional, metropolitan and multicultural churches, GCF-Toronto was launched in 2007 at the Centennial Community Centre and then progressed with a partnership with Canadian Baptists Ontario and Quebec to start GCF-Peel in 2008 and GCF-York in 2011 (Santos, 2013). Their vision contributed to development of GCF-Vancouver in 2010, GCF-Calgary in 2010 and GCF-Winnipeg in 2011 (Santos, 2013). This pattern of highly strategic initiatives is not common to all Christian immigrants, but the faith commitments and missionary capacity of recent immigrants should not be underestimated.

There are opportunities for long established churches to partner with recent newcomers if cultural obstacles to relationship can be overcome (denBok, 2013). As one example, access to meeting space is frequently mentioned as a current prayer concern of leaders in the New Canadian Church Planters discussion group facilitated by Tyndale Intercultural Ministry Centre. Both new churches and established churches are in a process of discovery to relate to their neighbourhoods. For new Canadians, decisions must be made on how to respond to this new environment, and for established congregations there is need to adjust to the change taking place around them.

Transition

There are both positive (opportunities) and negative (stresses) involved in transition. Many who move into the Toronto area do so for a new opportunity. I personally left rural south-western Ontario to move to the Greater Golden Horseshoe Area for post-secondary education and then later for ministry and employment opportunities. Several of my high school classmates followed a similar path, part of the urbanization trend within Canada.

Many of the challenges common to large, growing urban centres apply to Toronto. The cost of housing is a very basic concern that is receiving attention (Joy & Vogel, 2015), but without necessarily any solution in sight for the rising real estate costs. For 31.8% of Torontonians, more than 30% of their income is required for housing (Hiebert, 2015). This pressure contributes to movement across the region as people work out compromises between access to employment, services (health, education), friends, family and housing. These issues can compound the divide between rich and poor (Toronto Foundation, 2015).

One potentially hidden change that affects the lives of people with low income are the trends toward mixed-income housing where low income people must temporarily (or long term) move to a different neighbourhood. Gentrification (buying older, lower cost housing to be redeveloped for middle to upper income residents) contributes to these transitions and creates substantial change for many neighbourhoods (Walks & Marranen, 2008). Some of the more traditional low income neighbourhoods such as Parkdale (Slater, 2004) may have people who are among the working poor or living with some form of government financial assistance who are displaced by such processes to other parts of the city.

The current social experiment of mixed income housing (Harris, Dunn & Wakefield, 2015) is contributing to gentrification and relationships stretched across many neighbourhoods. While the intent may be to introduce middle-income professionals to avoid poverty ghettos, some of the people who have been displaced to inner suburbs retain significant connections to the core neighbourhoods and carry some of the social injustices and personal challenges with them. The inner suburbs can create new problems for these individuals and families as they may have less access to transit and do not have the same concentration of social services because this is such a recent shift within the city (Joy and Vogel, 2015).

For recently arrived international immigrants and refugees in Toronto, the learning curve can be challenging. They adjust to Canadian laws and learn how to access services (such as health care). Some may need to learn or improve their English, acquire new customs and make peace with the ups-and-downs of Lake Ontario weather. When asking recent immigrants questions about their experiences, I have been told that even basic advice on living in Canada can be helpful in their early stages of adjustment. When I asked a young man pursuing graduate education what I should tell pastors about helping immigrants, he enthusiastically told me to encourage them to ask questions like, "How are you?" and "Can I help you?" when someone is in their first six months in the country.

How is the Church in Toronto responding? While there is much learning yet needed for the Canadian church regarding how to respond to our multicultural society (Owusu, 2013; Janzen, Chapman & Watson, 2012; Sheffield, 2005), many congregations are responding. In 2014, five focus groups of congregational leaders (twenty in total) across the Greater Toronto Area (GTA) discussed why and how they supported newcomers to Canada (Chapman, Watson, Chang & Chang, 2014). What we found was that while some churches intentionally engaged in strategic visioning process to determine a direction and method for assisting immigrants, new initiatives often started from recognition of a need. This opportunity to understand a neighbour's need happened because of a personal relationship with someone who had recently arrived in Toronto (Chapman, Watson, Chang & Chang, 2014). It may start as simply as "How are you?" but progresses into a relationship which allows for a growing understanding of the challenges to be addressed (Watson & Chapman, 2014). Having friends in Toronto accelerates basic cultural learning that can address the daily necessities of life as well as contribute to simple friendship.

In addition to the transitions newcomers' experience, they change the city. Neighbourhoods change with the different waves of migration. Sometimes the change is gradual and sometimes it is relatively sudden. Degrees of cultural diversity exist across the city with different multicultural mixing taking place (Hiebert, 2015). At the personal level, differences among people from the same country of origin can be based on the different regions they lived in before migrating, when they immigrated, their primary reasons for migration or their personal investment in learning how to integrate (or conserve) their cultural values. This then plays out differently across generations. The typical distinction is made between the first generation arriving in Canada retaining substantial cultural elements while the second generation are connecting with a diverse spectrum of people their age as they integrate within the Canadian school system.[35] Canadian, multicultural society has sometimes been described as a mosaic, but perhaps a better image for Toronto is the kaleidoscope. Certain people may be holding on to their cultural identity (the fixed points in the kaleidoscope) but many are changing and mashing up with other cultures, lifestyles and perspectives around them.

The variety of cultural and spiritual identities in Toronto and the rate of change among neighbours and neighbourhoods could influence us toward suspicion of the person on the street. We do not know their story, their background or what communities they would claim as their own. Could we regard that person with curiosity, and anticipate that they might be moved by compassion like the Samaritan? Here the idea of Toronto as the Samaritan can raise our curiosity as to what their affiliations and convictions may be but with a positive, rather than fearful, approach to the person. Even though we assume they are different from ourselves, they may be the person God points out as an example of kingdom behaviour.

Jeff Christopherson (2012), a mission leader and former pastor in the Greater Golden Horseshoe Area, has suggested that one of the opportunities for building bridges in a setting like Toronto is to connect with women and men who already live out values of the kingdom of God without necessarily identifying as being people of faith. Working alongside these folks on a common project can create opportunities for deeper conversation. This approach allows us to walk alongside our neighbours and work on projects which bless our community. With respect to both responding to immigrants (Reimer, Janzen, Chapman, Watson & Wilkinson, 2016) and multi-generational Canadians within Golden Horseshoe neighbourhoods, there seems to be a religious or

---

[35] Among immigrants in Toronto, 54.6% were born abroad, 20.9% are second generation and 22.5% are at least third generation (Hiebert, 2015).

relational niche for congregations to serve within the city that may be difficult for other institutions to emulate (Janzen, Stobbe, Chapman & Watson, 2016; Stiller & Metzger, 2010). At some point we can have opportunity to share our own experience of life. If we are able to be transparent, the centrality of the gospel, experience of the love of God and ongoing practice of aligning ourselves with God's direction will be part of the conversation.

Interaction allows for listening and asking questions – conversation. Colonel Eleanor Shepherd, currently ministering in the highly multicultural Montreal Citadel of The Salvation Army provides a helpful focus for basic training in evangelism in the midst of complex communities: listening skills. She explains the value of listening first, which allows for discussion of our personal stories (Shepherd, 2010). Drawing upon the *politics of recognition* social theory of Canadian philosopher Charles Taylor, long time Golden Horseshoe resident and missiologist Dan Sheffield (2005) suggests this perspective can aid ministry in highly multicultural environments. Recognition of the other begins with listening. Listening does not replace proclamation of the gospel; relationships provide a context that allows for meaningful interaction.

Our family had been assisting with a church plant in a Greater Golden Horseshoe Area neighbourhood where the majority of the housing was low cost or subsidized rental units. A large portion of residents were both diverse and in transition. Newcomers to Canada could find housing until they had financial means to move into a preferred neighbourhood. The planters had built a wide diversity of friendships among a variety of Muslim, Hindu, Christian and agnostic people and a number of these friends would come to the community celebration worship services. It was after an Easter service in the local community centre that someone said, "Now I understand the Easter story. I have never heard it before. I was asking at ESL [English as a Second Language class] and no one could tell me." This young woman had arrived in Canada about three years earlier and we had enjoyed meeting with her and her husband to practice conversational English. That experience caused me to realize that it was possible in Canada for someone to never have heard the gospel. I knew that my friend had come from a Middle Eastern country that was under Islamic rule with very little Christian witness, but I had not anticipated that sharing life together would provide a first-time opportunity to share something so central to the Christian faith.

A City of Networks and Neighbourhoods

One of the challenges for understanding Toronto and imagining a faithful response is simply the size. The municipality has a population of 2.6 million and the census metropolitan area (CMA) has a population of 5.5 million which grew between the 2006 and 2011 census at a growth rate of 9 percent (Joy & Vogel, 2015). With the city of Toronto incorporating previous municipalities, there has been an amalgamation of distinctly different communities with distinct histories into one political body. Beyond the administrative expansion, Toronto represents the hub of a region that embraces a broad economic and residential area that is a regular part of the lives of many mobile residents who travel to workplaces in other municipalities.

The common use of terms such as "Greater Toronto Area," "Greater Toronto Hamilton Area" and "Golden Horseshoe" recognizes this mobility, and the interconnectedness of municipalities around the shore of Lake Ontario. The Ontario government incorporates the Toronto CMA with the regions of Halton, York, Peel, Durham, Peterborough, Kitchener-Waterloo, Guelph and St. Catherines-Niagara into the Greater Golden Horseshoe which has a total population of 7.5

million (Joy & Vogel, 2015). The growing commuter shadow that has enveloped Barrie to the north, Niagara to the south, Kitchener-Waterloo to the west and Peterborough to the east is represented by the GO train and bus system and demonstrates the draw of Toronto as an urban centre. This megaregion is "now alleged to be the fourth largest city region north of the Rio Grande" (Simmons & Bourne, 2011).

Because of the size and complexity of Toronto, it is helpful to explore the spirituality of the city in local context. The interrelated concepts of neighbourhoods and networks provide starting points for this exploration. Neighbourhoods can provide a geographic grid for understanding the city as a whole as well as natural entry points for interacting with neighbours. Networks allow for imagining the region as interconnected webs of relationships. They assist discovery of how people gather around specific interests and achieve a sense of belonging. Networks of relationships bridge between neighbourhoods and can extend transnationally because of the migration experiences of so many families connected to this region. We cannot simply label the stranger we encounter as a Samaritan and move on with life. We must get to know them in the context of their local experiences and relationships.

Neighbourhoods

Toronto is known as a city of neighbourhoods (City of Toronto, 2016) each with distinctive characteristics and providing housing for a variety of people groups (Tyndale Intercultural Ministry Centre, 2016). The history, topography, space, architecture and general aesthetics of the neighbourhood can provide opportunities for theological reflection and spiritual discernment (Hjalmarson, 2015; Smith, 2013). Neighbourhoods can be defined in the minds of Torontonians by the historic names of certain areas (China Town, Distillery District) or boundaries that have both geographic and social meaning, found in sayings like "the other side of the tracks."

Walking the neighbourhood and observing the surroundings can provide insight into the history and lifestyles of those who live there. Sometimes there are remarkable contrasts. I was part of a prayer walk in Etobicoke a few years ago when my friend and I turned down a dead end street. There was a park at the end of the street that was obstructed by a chain link fence where the entrance had been completely blocked. A large sign indicated that an official decision had been made at the municipal level to fence off the park. We asked a teen who was walking towards us (we assumed he was walking home from high school) if he knew why the entrance to the park had been closed. He said, "I guess the people over here, don't want the people over there coming onto their street." We thanked him and turned to leave. When we looked back he was on the other side of the fence, which he must have climbed in order to walk towards a group of apartment buildings. Contacts and observations in the neighbourhood tend to lead to new questions and over time a pattern of important themes can emerge from these interactions.

Demographics and other formal, data sources [36] can help to identify "blind spots" which may be difficult to determine through initial contacts or superficial conversation. However, it is not possible to engage fully in theological reflection and spiritual discernment by relying on statistics, actually listening to the stories of people is required. When I

---

[36] The city website both provides maps that illustrate the lattice of neighbourhoods (Toronto.ca/neighbourhoods) used for planning purposes and provides data on key indicators (Toronto.ca/wellbeing). The key indicators allow for initial exploration of trends based on the collected data, which may or may not conform to the perceptions of residents. Insight into some of the many different ethnicities, religious identities and countries of origin can be found on local sites such as: UReachToronto.com. Many of the commuter communities in the Greater Golden Horseshoe also have neighbourhood initiatives which can be found through their websites or speaking to community leaders. Statistics Canada's website also provides the ability to search for reports on specific communities or social issues. Certain mission agencies are able to provide analysis of demographics based on customized requests. Outreach Canada (outreach.ca) and Christian Direction (direction.ca) are examples of resource groups who provide these services.

was accompanying a school group for an urban intensive experience, we were given a tour of central Toronto by a sex trade worker. He started at the street corner where he was first picked up as a teen age runaway and finished the tour at the AIDS memorial where he anticipated his name would be engraved. He provided a window into a part of the city which I never could have glimpsed if I was only reviewing demographics.

Networks

Networks can exist within neighbourhoods (neighbours talking to each other over the fence), but extend far beyond the neighbourhood with commuting, telecommunications, video-over-internet and social media. In their book *Networked*, Lee Rainie & Barry Wellman (2012) argue that the combination of social networks, internet and mobile communication technologies are shaping an era of networked individualism. The individual shapes their own networks and the relationships in their personal networks shift over time according to their personal needs. A prominent feature of this social theory is that individuals are becoming more selective in how they form relationships. As relational networks provide opportunity for belonging and identification, they provide suggestions of the personal commitments or cultural and spiritual influences of our neighbours. The range of different issues, discussions and forms of activism that are available through digital media can allow development of relationships around very particular interests.

This shift has not necessarily reduced the amount of personal contact. Wellman studied relationships in Toronto's East York neighbourhood from 1968, observing the growth of the internet as a social phenomenon and considering its impact (Rainie & Wellman, 2012). He has concluded that nearby neighbours have only made up a small percentage (13%) of the primary networks of Torontonians from the beginning of his research (Rainie & Wellman, 2012). Consequently, the advent of the internet has not necessarily increased isolation or decreased neighbourliness in terms of local geography. The authors reference Pew Internet studies that indicate that online connections result in an increasing number of friends over time (Rainie & Wellman, 2012). The digital and mobile technologies "support participation in traditional settings such as neighborhoods, voluntary groups, churches, and public spaces" (Rainie & Wellman, 2012, p. 128).

Two examples of online interaction contributing to development of connections are Redeem the Commute and an e-mail settlement process sponsored by churches. These are illustrative of the many possibilities for making use of technology. Redeem the Commute is a smartphone app which allows people to engage in spiritual reflection during their GO train or bus commute and is contributing to formation of a new church in Durham region (Sim, 2014).

In two different research projects focused on how churches can assist migrants, I learned of church leaders who would initiate e-mail contact with migrants who are leaving their country before they had left. This contact allows them to answer questions about Canada, the settlement process and also assist them with developing relationships when they arrive in the region. The church leaders involved had also experienced the migration journey, had language ability and contacts in the country of origin.

A dramatic example of the impact of networks could be what I learned as I sat down with a couple who were engaged in outreach to sex trade workers in Toronto. They helped women transition off the streets and into addiction recovery programs and housing. When I explained the concept of networks to them and they had opportunity to map out some of their friends' connections, they realized that one important aspect of the women's lives was a lack of relationship to anyone outside of the sex trade. They essentially had one, closed, isolated, relational network. When some of the women embraced the grace available in Jesus and entered into new patterns of living, they also had to develop new relationships. They needed a church community, but it was not easy to find acceptance in an established congregation to form new networks of relationships.

Among immigrants to Toronto, their political interests, language, family, and friends who have remained in different countries along the migration journey can all provide a basis for the preservation and ongoing development of relationships. These transnational connections contribute to ongoing influence. Some recent immigrants may actively preserve their cultural identity, not only through selectively relating to individuals from their country of origin within Toronto but also through nurturing their transnational connections, personally investing their time and energy among their homeland and diaspora communities (through travel or communication technologies). Awareness of cultural and spiritual influence facilitated by relational networks can assist in missional engagement in neighbourhoods, particularly with recent immigrants (Watson, 2015). Globally connected individuals can act as gatekeepers not just with cultural or linguistic networks within the Greater Golden Horseshoe Area, but also to different regions around the world.

Addressing the Soul of the City

Do you know a Samaritan (in terms of the parable) in your neighbourhood? The metaphor is really only useful if it provides you with the ability to view the people in your networks of relationships differently. Being able to view the stranger you meet as someone who is valued by God, who has potential for redemptive action, changes our perspective on the city. We need to be able to discern, discuss and take action on the challenges that face a city as complex as Toronto, but the task is much different if we are viewing the people around us as potential allies rather than potential threats. We need to keep our eyes open, aware of the good and the bad, while praying and working towards God's transformation. Are there ways you can both partner with God and with your neighbours? Working together can help build the trust necessary to be able to engage in meaningful conversation.

It is good to reflect prayerfully and biblically on the soul of the city. God may reveal new aspects of our social environment. What will likely be the more important phase of the process is to consider our soul in the midst of the neighbourhoods and networks of the city. Are we in communion with God? Are we sensitive to the leading of the Holy Spirit? How can we identify what Jesus may be asking of us in the midst of the hurly-burly of everyday life as we rub shoulders with our neighbours (a very literal possibility during rush hour). What does it mean to carry the good news of Jesus in our souls and how does that affect the way we relate to others?

The relationships that are developed provide the richest opportunities to understand the soul of the city. The opinions, perspectives and stories provide insight into the hopes, dreams and fears that influence the spiritual atmosphere of our communities. The connections that develop can open whole new worlds of relationships, providing access to networks that weave throughout the region and extend around the world. The more connected we become, the more we recognize that our city is one node in the wider network of our country and our world.

References

Bibby, R.W. (2012). *A New Day: The Resilience and Restructuring of Religion in Canada.* Lethbridge: Project Canada Books. Retrieved from http://www.reginaldbibby.com/projectcanadabooks.html

Chapman, M., Watson, J., Chang, A. & Chang, N. (2014). *Site Report: Toronto: The Role of Churches in Immigrant Settlement and Integration.* Kitchener: Centre for Community Based Research. Retrieved from http://ureachtoronto.com/content/role-churches-immigrant-integration-settlement-project

Christopherson, J.A. (2012). *Kingdom Matrix.* Boise: Russell Media.

City of Toronto. (2016). Toronto Neighbourhoods List. Retrieved from http://www1.toronto.ca/wps/portal/contentonly?vgnextoid=100c861b9fdb1410VgnVCM10000071d60f89RCRD

Connor, P. (2014). *Immigrant Faith: Patterns of Immigrant Religion in the United States, Canada and Western Europe.* New York: New York University Press.

denBok, C. (2013). Church Planting by Immigrant Christians – And What the Rest of Us Can Learn. In Bowen, J.P. (Ed.), *Green Shoots Out of Dry Ground: Growing a New Future for the Church in Canada,* 79-92. Eugene: Wipf & Stock Publishers.

Evans, C. F. (1990). *Saint Luke.* London: SCM Press.

Harris, R., Dunn, J. and Wakefield, S. (2015, June). *A City on the Cusp: Neighbourhood Change in Hamilton Since 1970.* Toronto: Neighbourhood Change Research Partnership, Factor-Inwentash Faculty of Social Work, University of Toronto.

Hendrickx, H. (1986). *The Parables of Jesus.* San Francisco: Harper & Row Publishers, Inc.

Hiebert, D. (2015). *Ethnocultural Minority Enclaves in Montreal, Toronto and Vancouver*. Montreal: Institute for Research on Public Policy. (No. 52). Retrieved from http://irpp.org/research-studies/study-no52/

Hjalmarson, L. (2015). *No Home like Place*. Portland: Urban Loft Publishers.

Hultgren, A.J. (2000). *The Parables of Jesus*. Grand Rapids: Wm. B. Eerdmans Publishing Co.

Indigenous and Northern Affairs Canada. (2016). *Urban Aboriginal Peoples*. Retrieved from https://www.aadnc-aandc.gc.ca/eng/1100100014265/1369225120949

Janzen, R., Chapman, M., & Watson, J.W. (2012). Integrating Immigrants into the Life of Canadian Urban Christian Congregations: Findings from a National Survey. *Review of Religious Research 53*(4), 441–470.

Janzen, R., Stobbe, A., Chapman, M. & Watson, J.W. (2016). Canadian Christian churches as Partners in Immigrant Settlement and Integration. *Journal of Immigrant and Refugee Studies*. doi: 10.1080/15562948.2015.1123792

Joy, M. & Vogel, R.K. (2015). Toronto's Governance Crisis: A Global City Under Pressure. *Cities, 49*, 35-52.

Lo, L. (2008). DiverCity Toronto: Canada's Premier Gateway City. In M. Price, and L. Benton-Short (Eds.), *Migrants to the Metropolis: The Rise of Immigrant Gateway Cities*, 97–127. Syracuse: Syracuse University Press.

Owusu, S. "To All Nations:" The Distinctive Witness of the Intercultural Church. In J.P. Bowen (Ed.), *Green Shoots Out of Dry Ground:*

Growing a New Future for the Church in Canada, 115-126. Eugene: Wipf & Stock Publishers.

Parsons, M.C. (1995). *Luke*. Grand Rapids: Baker Academic.

Rainie, L. & Wellman, B. (2012). *Networked*. Cambridge: The MIT Press.

Reimer, S., Janzen, R., Chapman, M., Watson, J. & Wilkinson, M. (2016). Christian Churches and Immigrant Support in Canada. *Review of Religious Research*. doi: 10.1007/s13644-016-0252-7

Ringe, S.H. (1995). *Luke*. Louisville: Westminster John Knox Press.

Santos, N.F. (2013). What's a Missionary Doing in Canada? In Bowen, J.P. (Ed.), *Green Shoots Out of Dry Ground: Growing a New Future for the Church in Canada*, 97-110. Eugene: Wipf & Stock Publishers.

Scott, B.B. (1990). *Hear Then the Parable*. Minneapolis: Augsburg Fortress.

Shafer, B.C. (2014). *Cosmopolis Toronto: Photographing the World, One Torontonian at a Time*. Retrieved from http://cosmopolistoronto.com/

Sheffield, D. (2005). *The Multicultural Leader*. Toronto: Clements Publishing.

Shepherd, E. (2010). *More Questions than Answers*. Eugene: Wipf and Stock Publishers.

Sim, R. (2014). *Redeem the Commute*. Retrieved from http://www.redeemthecommute.com/

Simmons, J. & Bourne, L.S. (2013, August). The Canadian Urban System in 2011: Looking Back and Projecting Forward. Toronto: Cities Centre, University of Toronto.

Slater, T. (2004). Municipally Managed Gentrification in South Parkdale, Toronto. *The Canadian Geographer 48*(3), 303–325.

Smith, G. (2013). Reading Your Community: Towards an Authentic Encounter with a Canadian Context. In J.P. Bowen (Ed.), *Green Shoots Out of Dry Ground: Growing a New Future for the Church in Canada*, 219-238. Eugene: Wipf & Stock Publishers.

Stiller, K. & Metzger, W. (2010). *Going Missional*. Winnipeg: Word Alive Press.

Thurén, L. (2014). *Parables Unplugged*. Minneapolis: Fortress Press.

Toronto Foundation. (2015). *Toronto's Vital Signs Report 2015*. Retrieved from https://torontofoundation.ca/sites/default/files/OP-TVS%202015-Full-Report-PRINTING.pdf

Tyndale Intercultural Ministry Centre. (2016). *Toronto's Diverse People Groups*. Retrieved from http://ureachtoronto.com/content/torontos-diverse-people-groups

Walks, R.A. & Maaranen, R. (2008, May). The Timing, Patterning & Forms of Gentrification & Neighbourhood Upgrading in Montreal, Toronto & Vancouver 1961 to 2001. Toronto: Cities Centre, University of Toronto.

Watson, J.W. (2015). *Interaction Mapping*. Ph.D dissertation. School of Intercultural Studies, Fuller Theological Seminary, Pasadena, CA.

Watson, J.W. & Chapman, M. (2014, September 9). Caring for the Stranger in Our Midst. *Good Idea!* Retrieved from http://institute.wycliffecollege.ca/2014/09/caring-for-the-stranger-in-our-midst/

Wilkinson, M. (2006). *The Spirit Said Go: Pentecostal Immigrants to Canada*. New York: Peter Lang.

Hjalmarson

CHAPTER NINE

Ottawa, Ontario
Richard Long

On New Year's Eve, 1857 the citizens of Ottawa (formerly Bytown) were pleasantly surprised that Queen Victoria had chosen their muddy lumber town as the permanent capital of Upper and Lower Canada. The process had taken 17 years and by-passed the major urban centers and former capital sites of York (Toronto), Kingston, Montreal and Quebec City. Ottawa is located at the convergence of three rivers, the Ottawa, the Rideau, and the Gatineau. The new name, chosen in 1855, refers to the local Aboriginal name "Odawa" meaning "Trade."

Ottawa was deemed the best site for a capital for two predominant reasons. Firstly, it was distant enough from the U.S. border and the risk of invasion, and secondly it was situated on the border of the Anglophone and Francophone provinces that constantly vied for pre-eminence. The themes of safety and compromise, or to put it more positively - stability and accommodation - would shape the city from that time on. In this chapter we are going to look at 7 aspects of Ottawa that shape the soul of this city.

Two Ottawas

Ten years after the Queen's decision, with the dawn of Confederation and the arrival of politicians, and an emerging civil service, the town had more than doubled in size to 18,000. In 2016 the population was 900,000 living on a huge footprint of 2790 sq km that included 13 former municipalities. Another 300,000 who live across the river in Gatineau, Quebec, have a distinct culture from the rest of that province and contribute a significant percentage of the federal workforce. In total, according to the Census, the Metropolitan Area consists of 1.2 million persons.

A long-time resident of Ottawa describes the city this way, "There are still two Ottawas - the lumber town and the government town." The local phrase "Below the Queensway" describes well this separation as it refers to the downtown core north of the major freeway, where most of the government offices are located away from the rest of urban life. These two realities – government hub and lumber town - are still evident as 18-wheeler logging trucks crawl in a zigzag pattern through the downtown streets, just blocks from Parliament Hill, attempting to cross the only major traffic bridge to the Quebec side.

In the 150 years since Confederation it is the government side that has won the identity battle. Lumber mills and their workers were shut down or moved on. Very little replaced them until the hi-tech boom of the 1980's arrived to the west in the mushrooming new suburb city of Kanata. But in the early 2000's many of those jobs were eliminated and only recently has there been some rebuilding of that sector. With 130,000 federal civil servants living in the national capital region, plus the employers at other levels of government; the RCMP, the military, the embassies, the myriad NGO staff, and the secondary companies who are financed by government contracts; almost everyone is supported out of federal coffers.

The lumber town has become a proud capital. Taxpayer's money has funded world class art galleries, national performance centers, multiple museums and all the trappings of high-culture, including a new opera house under construction in 2016. Universities and colleges have sprung up to train a highly educated civil service. Ottawa has the highest number of post-graduate degrees per capita in the country. It is the place to live if you want to influence a nation.

The Political Powers

The cityscape of downtown Ottawa is striking. There are no tall skyscrapers like those that crowd the inner core of Canada's other major cities. This low horizon is due to the by-law that prohibits any building from exceeding the height of the Peace Tower on Parliament Hill (New by-laws are allowing taller condos at a good distance from the urban core). The political powers literally look down on the rest of the city.

Political power defines Ottawa; after all it is a capital city. Tom White of Frontline Ministries, has some helpful insights into how this affects churches and ministries. He has been traveling the world helping city-reaching movements for over 30 years and has been a great resource to the churches in Ottawa. Tom has led pastors' prayer summits and has sat with Ottawa city leadership teams on eight occasions over the span of 15 years. Quite often he has shared an insight which he calls "Capital City Syndrome." It is something he sees in Washington, London, Seoul and numerous other places.

White notes that the most common similarity for all capital cities is the aptitude for bureaucracy. Civil servants have the most coveted jobs in this society. Some in Ottawa are third or fourth generation workers. They are instinctively trained to obey the many rules and procedures imposed upon them. Compliance is rewarded with a steady climb over a long career to a retirement at the six figure level with benefits. Government work moves forward cautiously and therefore slowly; protocol matters.

One new church-planting pastor remarked that he had never been in a place where the first question from a newcomer was, "Where can I read the church constitution?" The churches of Ottawa are full of civil servants. Pastors learn to move forward incrementally in order to get their new ideas implemented. Board members are experts in making sure that all policies and procedures are complied with as decisions get made. In an atmosphere where process is really important, spiritual leaders who are successful learn how to be patient and work for the long term win with gradual momentum. Building consensus is critical.

There are not just three levels of government in Ottawa as there are in most Canadian cities. Citizens of the capital have a complicated and intertwined relationship with a fourth, non-elected entity called the National Capital Commission (NCC). Only in early 2016 did this powerful council agree to allow the two mayors of Ottawa and Gatineau to sit in their midst, yet without voting privileges. Until very recently all decisions were made in secret by a committee appointed by a federal cabinet minister.

The constant reminder of the NCC's power and presence is everywhere. The NCC controls most of the visible landmarks of the city – Parliament Hill, the museums, the monuments, the parks, the sprawling parklands, the Rideau Canal and many institutional buildings. While local citizens are proud and grateful for so much of this work there are also the lasting challenges.

The National Capital Commission's most enduring legacy is what the original designer called "the emerald necklace." The greenbelt vision of the Parisian architect Jacques Gréber in 1950 was intended to limit urban growth to the interior, allowing for a population of 500,000. Working after World War II with the empowerment of Prime Minister Louis St-Laurent, Gréber's ideas still gridlock the city over sixty years later.

The Greenbelt is a parable about well-intentioned vision, political power struggles, bureaucracy and development into the 21st century. Protection of a large urban forest, farms and wetlands was possible only because of government expropriation in the 1960's. It has provided Ottawans with 203.5 sq km of hiking and skiing trails, fresh air and other ecological benefits. It has not created the tight urban environment that Jacques Gréber envisioned. His estimate of a half million population by year 2000 was arrived at in 1970. Already the suburban cities of Kanata (west), Barrhaven (south) and Orleans (east) had begun their expansion outside the greenbelt. By 2016 they have each mushroomed to over 100,000 and continue to gobble up farmland on all sides.

Multiple roads crisscross the greenbelt, swollen with CO_2 exhaling cars and buses which have to make an extra long commute to work. The ecological cost in air quality has been huge. Who can measure the human toll on families with long and frustrating traffic congestion? The suburb cities have very little industry and serve primarily as bedroom communities for the government jobs downtown. There was no plan to make them self-sustaining with their own industries and employers. The current transit system is built to take people to that core and not to the few light industrial areas within the region. A new light rail system began to be built in 2014, but has been re-focused on serving the city core and won't arrive until 2030 for those who need it the most in the commuter suburb cities. Jacques Gréber (1882 – 1962) haunts every corner of Ottawa and its suburbs and daily frustrates every citizen.

That said, and in spite of the immediate need, this is a city that prefers the safe and stable approach. It translates to the Christian culture as well. It is said that the political spirit wars against the prophetic spirit. While there have been small revivals, the preferred method of growth is slow and steady. Charismatic expressions have not thrived. Though there are large Pentecostal congregations, the atmosphere in the worship services are almost identical to their Conservative Evangelical brethren.

More broadly, and another testament to stability, religion is expected to maintain its gradually dwindling place in society. The Jewish citizenry have always been tiny but careful in a city with some historic anti-Semitism. They number only 1.2 percent compared to much larger populations in Montreal, Toronto, and Winnipeg.

The quickly growing Muslim population which now makes up 6% of the city has learned how to adapt to political correctness in recent years. The Ottawa Muslim Association recently asked for an imam educated in the U.S. They rejected a Saudi-trained imam after a short tenure who had already replaced an extremist Libyan imam, later cited with encouraging terrorism. Samy Metwally, who arrived in July 2011 to become the new imam at The Ottawa Mosque, has shown himself to be a well adjusted Western-style leader. He regularly stands at podiums with the leading Jewish Rabbi, the Archbishop, and Protestant leaders to encourage harmony among faith groups.

Though 45% of the population is baptized Roman Catholic, the few people in the pews underline the fact that from the Prime Minister on down, a government-dominated culture doesn't expect the Church to have much to say or contribute to the life of normal people. In fact it is expected to stay silent on any issue that the Government considers is in its own purview. Ottawa was rocked in March, 2008 when the newly appointed Catholic Archbishop Prendergast warned he would not allow his priests to serve communion to Catholic politicians who were pro-abortion and advocated euthanasia. Local media castigated him for not understanding his place in society.

The French Element

If the first prominent duality in Ottawa is the government hub and timber town, the second is the presence of Francophones. It might be the street signs that begin with "Rue" or "Chemin" or it might be the ubiquity of Quebec license plates. Downtown Ottawa is clogged with Gatineau city buses picking up the workforce that lives across the river in the province of Quebec.

The eastern half of the city, including the eastern edge city of Orleans has a well developed separate Francophone culture including schools, college, shops, and community associations. One delights in hearing Quebecois accents in any gathering. It is often accompanied by a more visible passion in conversations about almost any subject. A deep commitment to family and culture are strengths of this part of the population. Among Protestants there is a clear weakness in learning how to reach into this culture. While there may be larger Francophone African and Haitian congregations, it is obvious that Evangelical and Charismatic churches are small among the French-Canadian population.

There is also a very strong French influence in the halls of government because of their community's adept bilingual abilities. Over 30% of Ottawans are fluent in both languages but it is the Francophones who have made more effort than the English population to work in a second language. Bilingual ability is expected in many other sectors including much of the retail industry. Among Anglophones there is a constant low level of animosity about that preference by employers.

Bridge-building: A Sign of the Kingdom

For over twenty years the municipal governments of Ottawa and Gatineau have been trying to build another bridge over the river, with hopes of taking the lumber trucks and other heavy traffic away from the crowded downtown. Environmental research and feasibility studies abound for numerous preferred routes, yet no consensus has been found to date. Ottawa is a city of politicians, yet bridge building is still very difficult.

In contrast the bridge-building between believers of different church backgrounds has been going along steadily for many years as trust among spiritual leaders has increased. Love Ottawa, the current expression of collaborative and prayerful unity has seen a dramatic increase of activity and impact in very recent years. Working under the umbrella of One Way Ministries, a twenty year old ministry that has dedicated itself to serving leaders, the Love Ottawa team has multiplied numerous teams and initiatives since 2012.

Pastors of all denominational backgrounds find themselves working on cooperative ventures both locally and city-wide. Projects are sometimes focused on the one hundred and two local neighbourhoods that comprise the city or perhaps targeted at one of the many different people groups.

Just a few examples of coordinated outreach can be listed. There is a Refugee Response Team to coordinate reception of Syrians fleeing the Middle East, a Gangs and Guns mentoring initiative to provide coaching to vulnerable young men. There is Friends for Dinner – an outreach to the nine thousand international students who study at the 4 universities and colleges in Ottawa, Dig and Delve - a post-modern apologetics approach aimed at equipping and speaking to the 20-somethings in the city. Then there is The Big Give – a city-wide extreme generosity event that over 65 congregations support, to provide a message of kindness in June each year across the neighbourhoods.

Like many of Canada's cities, Ottawa has been welcoming new Canadians for several decades. There are over 40 new churches who are led by internationals and who have created their own support system called the International Pastors and Leaders Forum. This group now regularly interacts with the more established churches. In early 2017 many of these pastoral couples were part of the 100 leaders who made the annual trek to a winter pastors' prayer retreat that has been happening for 19 years.

Internationals have arrived in 4 major categories in recent years. The largest immigrant group for many years was Lebanese who arrived in the 1980's with the devastation of their homeland. They found the bilingualism of Ottawa easy to adjust to with their second languages of French and English. Most of these newcomers were from the Christian side of the Lebanese population and have built large Orthodox and Catholic congregations that operate independently from the other churches.

Ottawa doesn't have a huge Chinese population, and thus has a smaller "Chinatown'" but you will find several large evangelical Mandarin-speaking congregations in that area. A Chinese ministerial has grown up to serve the dozen congregations that are now spread all over the region. These churches grow quietly but quickly and are effective in reaching out to the many mainland Chinese students who attend the universities in the city.

A smaller but vibrant Filipino contingent are planting churches and taking a strong role in the life of the larger church. The annual Global Day of Prayer on the Pentecost weekend is anchored by the hundreds of Filipinos who gather on the steps of Parliament.

Not to be underestimated are the African peoples. A strong tendency among Africans especially from the central and eastern nations of that continent is to settle near the source of political power in the country that they adopt. There are shopping areas and pockets of business that have a concentration of African entrepreneurs. This same strong initiative is seen in the church community. Ottawa has many small African congregations led by tent-makers who establish the kind of congregations that they are familiar with back home both in language and theology. Some of these have become fast growing enterprises, outpacing the growth of the other congregations in the city.

Prayer Saturation

The "right hand" of Love Ottawa is aptly named Pray Ottawa. Every working team raised up for an outreach purpose is required to have a prayer strategy to cover their work. The point of this emphasis is to remind leaders that they are dependent on the supernatural help of God to accomplish anything of eternal value.

Christians have been praying together interdenominationally on a consistent basis for decades in Ottawa. Numerous new opportunities are now arising. Along with organized prayer walks, usually in high need areas or in neighbourhoods for future church planting, training for local congregations helps others learn how to "pray with their feet."

Probably the most significant effort is the weekly "Prayer Point." For over 5 years a short weekly email has been created around a particular theme or need, landing in the inbox of 900 pastors and prayer leaders. The churches of Ottawa literally have the opportunity to pray on the same page each week. Who can measure the impact of over 250 weeks of continuous focused prayer?

There are other regular events for those believe in the power of prayer. Easter morning sees believers gather on the steps of Parliament to celebrate the risen Christ, a tradition that is now over 30 years old. A few weeks later at Pentecost the city comes together for a Global Day of Prayer again on Parliament Hill. This event is led by international pastors and thus brings an exuberance rarely seen in that location.

Every fall for the last seven years, 400-500 Christians from all backgrounds gather for the Ottawa Prayer Breakfast. It is an "honour" event that expresses gratitude to the Mayor, City Councilors, Police, Fire and Emergency Service workers. Beyond the prayer that is offered on that occasion the participants leave with a bookmark with names of all civic, provincial, and federal leaders who they can remember in prayer throughout the year.

In 2005 the National House of Prayer was launched in Ottawa under the leadership of Rob and Fran Parker. It hosts prayer teams every week who come from all across the nation to meet and pray with their local MPs and Senators. The facility has been a great catalyst for local congregations to think more seriously about the impact of prayer. At the beginning of 2015 a new city-focused effort began a daily schedule of consistent prayer for Ottawa itself. The "Burning Hearts House of Prayer" has created a new impetus and vision for reaching the city and is likely only the first of other new prayer houses to arise in the years ahead.

Catholics and Evangelicals have been learning to walk together for over 20 years, starting with the March for Jesus public praise events in the mid 90's, then with collaboration for a Billy Graham Crusade in 1998. There has been easy friendship and mutual worship and prayer between Charismatic leaders from both groups throughout all those years. Leaders have committed to speak well of each other and guard each other's positions. Bridge building across this historic divide also usually means English and French Christians are learning to appreciate each other and pray for the Spirit's work amongst one other.

Renewed Catholics

From its very beginnings, with both a French and English population, Ottawa has been a place where Protestants and Catholics have learned to live side-by-side. Outside of Quebec, Ottawa has the largest percentage of Catholic population of any of Canada's larger cities. Catholics have a proud history in the city as evidenced by large cathedrals, many hospitals and institutions, and 103 parishes.

One of the best kept secrets in the closing years of the 20th century was the story of the emergence of a new Roman Catholic order based out of the St. Mary's Parish in the Dow's Lake area of Ottawa. The Companions of the Cross was formed with the Archbishop's blessing in 1982, and soon became the fastest growing order of priests in North America. They were birthed out of a strong Charismatic Catholic ministry in that parish church and have continued to produce priests who are both Charismatic and Evangelical.

In this environment it is not surprising that other kinds of life has been erupting among Catholics in Ottawa. In 2005, a national university outreach ministry moved their centre from Saskatchewan to the city. Catholic Christian Outreach is the largest student ministry on the campuses of Ottawa's universities. It also has workers in 11 other campuses across Canada focusing on evangelizing students. Not to be forgotten is a national ministry to high school campuses across the nation. Net Ministries utilizes young men and women who devote a year to being trained and then deployed to lead Catholic secondary school students into a relationship with Christ. They are based in the eastern suburb of Orleans.

Perhaps the strongest indication that a renewal is happening among Ottawa Catholics is the New Evangelization Summit. In its third year in 2017 it held another sold-out two day conference focused on training Catholics how to bring a vibrant witness to the world. Through a "live" video feed they beamed the conference to 30 other sites in North America and reached 5000 attendees. Ottawa has become the epicenter of a new gospel-empowered movement that is resourcing and inspiring Catholic leaders on the rest of the continent.

Going it Alone

As one leaves the densely populated Golden Triangle of western Lake Ontario and makes their way easterly along the 401 highway, it becomes apparent that the capital city of Ottawa seems to be in the middle of nowhere. That was Queen Victoria's intention apparently.

This isolation has created an environment where Ottawa residents look to their fellow citizens for understanding and support. As the second largest urban centre in the province and the fourth largest metropolitan complex in Canada, the national capital has developed its own identity. Many local church leaders have come to the conclusion that they should not depend on a national denominational office some place far away to help them. Pastors look across the denominational lines for mutual support and common vision. So for example, in the area of evangelism and church planting, there is a growing consensus that the Church in Ottawa needs to take responsibility for its own growth. A city-wide, city-owned vision for bringing the gospel to every neighbourhood has to be developed and sustained by the Christian believers that live in the capital.

Ottawa is a city that you can get your mind around. It is small enough that you can drive across it in 45 minutes, but big enough to have an IKEA, 70 Tim Horton's coffee shops, and all the other regular evidences of modern urban civilization. It's a knowable city. The Christian community, especially because of the many varied opportunities to connect, has become quite tight-knit and committed to working together. CHRI a strong local Christian radio station, and "Spur Ottawa" - a new digital magazine, are bolstering this unity.

The Soul of the City

Ottawa's proudest ongoing monument to its historical and global significance is the Rideau Canal. Perhaps the canal is the soul of the city. It is the living, moving heart of Ottawa as it flows north from the southern leafy suburbs to the sides of Parliament Hill. In 2007 the Rideau Canal was officially designated a UNESCO World Heritage Site. It was Colonel John By (from which Bytown received its name) who in 1826 began this ambitious project to connect Lake Ontario with the barracks on the Ottawa River 202 km away. This required the clearing of forests, blasting of large rock formations, and drainage of hectares of mosquito-infested marshlands. Many of the workers came down with malaria and over 500 died from the disease as they sweated and dug to incarnate this grand idea.

When it was finally completed in 1832, with a 60% overrun on its budget, it was soon to be obsolete. The railway was about to arrive and the modern central station across from the future Canadian Pacific hotel would eclipse everything that the original planners had designed. Yet the Rideau Canal has survived and thrived. Not as a boating system - for very few vessels ply their way along its locks - but as a tourist attraction. What might surprise Colonel By the most is that the canal is most popular in the sub-zero winter months.

Ottawa claims the title of the second coldest capital in the world. Only Ulan Bator in Mongolia bests the frozen winters of Canada's capital. But Ottawans don't hibernate; a government has to be run. So the canal has been turned into the world's longest skateway. A full 13 km of skating pleasure is enjoyed and boosted by the citizens of Ottawa. The annual Winterlude festival in mid February attracts over a million visitors to the Rideau Canal when most other Canadian cities would be hunkering down for the winter.

The Soul of the City

This is the epitome of Ottawa. A malaria-infested swamp, that at great cost was meant to become a place of transportation and commerce, which never fulfilled its stated purpose. When that short-sighted vision was lost, it was transformed by the imagination of local citizens into a commercially successful world-class place of delight and recreation. The people of Ottawa have learned to adapt the large dreams of outsiders and translate them into a realistic and enjoyable way of life. Perhaps that's the legacy of something deeper than the canal, a real soul. Ottawans continue to make the most of the grandiose dreams of the politicians who come and go, as they seek to be a city that sets a pace for the nation both culturally and spiritually.

Hjalmarson

CHAPTER TEN

Montreal, Quebec
Dominic Ruso

What our Post-Christian Contexts reveal about the Church
Montréal & Surrounding Urban Vitality

The pioneering preacher and Methodist leader John Wesley once said that he looked upon the whole world as his parish. What Wesley could not have anticipated is that if we want to get honest about reaching the world we must begin with getting serious about engaging the diversity of our cities. Urban reengagement with focused attention on religious diversity and spiritual vitality has never been so important. Moreover, it is no longer sufficient to view intersection with our cities solely as an evangelistic pursuit. Instead, projects like this remind us that something much more urgent is at stake. We need a fresh outlook to explore how our culture shapes our ideas, how numerous disciplines inform and form the people we are becoming, and how both of these realities underpin the cities we are building. Hence, this invitation to contribute to this work was as a joyful reminder that new voices are emerging to provide a fresh outlook for the future of Christ-centered mission in our cities.

Montréal: The 60's and a new Vision concerning Identity

Montréal[37] is Canada's second largest city. Originally named Ville Marie, this city's roots reveal a long and complicated relationship to matters of Christian identity and civic responsibility. It is impossible to miss how the most symbolic streets and corridors of the city are associated with references to Roman Catholic saints and biblical characters. For example, Saint Catherine Street, a street symbolic of the downtown epi-center of this city remains a popular hotspot for tourists. This common practice of naming streets, parks and buildings after figures from scripture is indicative of the place of the Christian history in the early formation of the city. Moreover, this provides a reminder of how early Roman Catholic leaders focused on seeing the progress of the city as a tribute to God's faithfulness and the influence of the church. (Sancton, 1984, 1).

While an admirable vision, the rich religious heritage of this city has not slowed the pace of change in a metropolis like Montréal. A recent report by the *Quebec Human Rights Commission* reveals people living in Montréal have changed their tune as it relates to questions around the role of religion and in its relevance in our world.[38] While these present realities are complex, the city's relationship to Christianity has been tumultuous and anyone serious about understanding the spiritual climate which forms and informs the soul of this city must recall some key moments in history.

The 1960's were monumental years for those desiring to make sense of how religion and public life might contribute to a diversely

---

[37] Montréal is a reference to Mont Royal. A strategic area in the city which now has a park and the famous cross on top of the mountain. No building in Montréal is allowed to be taller than the famous cross found on Mont Royal.

[38] A 2015 report discussed in the Montréal Gazette noted, "43 per cent of respondents said you should be suspicious of anyone who openly expresses their religion." http://Montréalgazette.com/news/how-widespread-is-islamophobia-in-quebec.

charged context. The world exhibition called *Expo '67* brought to the fore the diversity of the world for a growing Montréal. For many Canadians this was the first time they came to visit the city brining them face to face with its bilingual flare and passionate fervor for life. My family still talks about the visionary zeal of those years, remembering how many immigrants celebrated their customs as part of *Expo*. While this cultural fair of diversification seemed to unite many living in the city and the larger province, another more complicated shift threatened to tear things apart.

Often called The Quiet Revolution/*Révolution Tranquille*, the 1960's are symbolic of a drastic shift in societal identity. The decade was steered by a new individualism, focused on the need for new ideals, calling into question the role of religious beliefs and public life. Especially for Francophones, the Roman Catholic Church, up to this point, had been an all-consuming force. Hence, the desire for change was often seen as a break from the old narratives of the past. While interpretations vary, comprehensive governmental reforms associated with this 'revolution' remain formative for the reshaping of Montréal religious history.

As part of the discussion there emerged a strong review of the role of the church (primarily Roman Catholic Church) in public life, education and many other social programs - programs often governed by church leaders. For someone who grew up in Montréal following the Quiet Revolution it remains difficult to fully grasp the struggles and feelings that many experienced during the so called oppressive years of church. All that to say that in 1960, change was in the air. Furthermore, the changes in the city of Montréal coincided with significant conversations of change within the Roman Catholic Church. Moreover, the 60's are forever associated with the Catholic Church's Second Vatican council.[39]

The new questions that surfaced following the turbulent 60's sought to clarify a new vision for Quebec which would come to bear on its largest city, Montréal. The ensuing conversation sought to realign the city with the values of modernity: progress, prosperity, and personal fulfillment. The new outlook also required revisiting the place of religion and its impact on the identity of Quebecers living in a new diversified context. Since the Church had come to be seen as oppressive and domineering, many believed that the only way to experience the fullness of human flourishing required denouncing the church. Accordingly, the decisions that followed made it clear that if religion was to have any function in the future of the city, it should be kept private and apart from the new governmental structures.

The subsequent battles about identity led to aggressive anticlerical sentiments which explain much of today's religious debates. Baum, a leading theologian on many of these issues, writes, "The Quiet Revolution also initiated the process of secularization... [a process] to replace the religious story that had defined Quebec's past identity with the secular self-definition of a people eager to discover its power, talent, and originality. (Baum, 2014, 10). It is impossible to understand the soul of this city without an understanding of how the 60's revitalized the individualistic spirit within the heart of *les Quebecois,* fostering the pursuit of a new vision of self-identity devoid of ecclesial authority.

These important transitions did not mean that people suddenly stopped attending Mass or believing in God, yet a powerful movement began. This movement led to today's existential vacuity, impacting our

---

[39] While space does not permit, these years were also formative for the Roman Catholic Church as Vatican II was in session from 1962-65.

understanding of personal identity and 'meaning making' in the public square. A recent French documentary entitled *L'Heureux Naufrage*, (Fortunate Shipwreck) provides an exploration of the consequences related to faith and religion. The Quiet Revolution generated new questions from people living in Quebec. One interviewee, reflecting on the present predicament, states, "We are probably living in the only era where a boy asks his father, "What's the meaning of life?" and the father remains silent. (Schmitt, 2014). The loss of influence once found in the 'trusted' practices of the church birth a leadership vacuum founded on the human hunger for identity and a meaningful life.

When Religious Tensions Get Personal

As a practitioner engaging with these realities it is my personal conviction that any pastoral leader who desires to understand the larger context of Quebec's religious past must remain sensitive to such issues. Having grown up in Montréal during the 70's and 80's and having recently returned after a 16 year stretch serving in diverse churches abroad, I remember how the shifts mentioned above played a role in my own faith journey.

As the son of Italian immigrants I remember attending Roman Catholic mass as a young boy and can appreciate the role the church played in those early years. Our faith as Roman Catholics was linked to deep family history and the heritage of parents and grandparents. You can imagine the shock when, due to a variety of events, my mother started attending a Protestant church with Pentecostal leanings. To help situate this within Quebec's larger dynamics Richard Lougheed remarks on the growing animosity between Protestants and Catholics even before the 1960's, noting that tension revealed how both groups, "... felt threatened by the other's existence [and] in the 19th Century both continued to strongly project their views and dispute the errors of the other." (Lougheed, 2011, 99). Although today it is encouraging to observe the learning that has led to a more amiable relationship between Protestants and Catholics, the previous experience was dominated by pain and anger.

This change in religious affiliation for my mother, and eventually my brother and I, was seen as a deep violation of our Roman Catholic heritage. In addition, this desire to find a new expression for pursing our questions about belief in God meant that we no longer found our identity as firstly Roman Catholic Christians, anchored within our European and French identity. Instead, we were *individual* Canadians seeking out truth wherever it may lead us. This radical step embodied the spirit of a new secularized era of religious exploration, a spirit that remains to this day. What followed for me was a long and circuitous path that caused me to wrestle with family history and discerning my vocational path.

This personal experience fits as a symbolic reminder of the tensions of religious life in Quebec. Hence, the city of Montréal must be seen as a diversely secular urban space inviting individualistic explorations of faith. My present learning as a church planter reveals a growing level of dissatisfaction when churches use forceful tactics, attempting to colonize the complex stories of pilgrimage. This new secular space informs us of the unique qualities and currents that have forged the dynamic milieu of this city, and the need for new leadership models to manage its post-Christian context.

The tension underlying those who see themselves as Roman Catholics and those who embrace a Protestant form of Christianity must be explored gently yet intentionally if the good news will be embraced in the city. The wisdom of missiologist Lesslie Newbigin shines clear when stating, "it is on the mission field that the sense of shame about disunity has been most powerfully at work-" (Newbigin, 1961, 22). This confusion lingers for many who grew up in now a secularized context, unsure about how these so called Christian families, with years of religious discord, fit the larger picture of Quebec society.

An Emerging Spiritualized Secularism

The growing diversity of Canada's urban centers require an honest discussion about how religious upheaval has shaped some of the major shifts we are experiencing today. While the term 'secular' is a pregnant term, it is most often understood as referring to a culture adapting to new non-religious approaches to civil life. In 2015, political leaders from Quebec's *Parti Quebecois* explored the theme of secularism and the way it may impact forms of religious terrorism and radicalization.[40] These debates put Montréal at the forefront of the important balancing act between religious freedom and social responsibility. Hence it seems that Quebec is an emerging experiment in a type of secularism which is trying to hold in tension spiritual fervor, religious diversity and social responsibility.

Harvey Cox has observed, "scholars of religion refer to the current metamorphosis in religiousness with phrases like 'the move to horizontal transcendence'... as the rediscovery of the sacred in the immanent, *the spiritual within the secular*." (Cox, 2009, 2). In Montréal, conversations about what Christian flourishing means must take into consideration how a secular culture engages with spiritual matters. While there remains a cognitive dissonance about linking both 'secular' and 'spiritual' together we are learning that this is exactly the vibe of the emerging intellectual space of our time. With this come new questions concerning spiritual matters which push outside the traditional bounds

---

[40] http://Montréal.ctvnews.ca/philosopher-says-secularism-push-could-create-new-divisions-in-quebec-society-1.2201383.

of ecclesial guidance. The new and changing post-Christian environment shaped *by* the church and the years of religious infighting has weakened the church's voice of influence for many who now see themselves as secular *and* spiritual. These realities have been defined as the new post-secular approach which include a universal longing causing spiritual reawakened. James K. Smith has noted the need to recognize the false assumptions of modernity which promised the triumph of science producing a secular world without religion. His research is foundational in exploring how our daily 'liturgies' and practices in our 'post-secular' world informs *how* we come to believe not just *that* we believe. (Smith, 2006).

Another challenge which is becoming increasingly clear is that many churches have never grown beyond the simplistic 'conversion narratives,' which do not do just to the complex ways of belief in a post-secular context. The old arguments that pigeon hole non-believer into categories we can preach about will no longer carry weight. Consequently, the missional conversations required for reaching those disinterested in church, yet open to spiritual conversations, must move us beyond finger pointing within the walls of Christian communities. Denominations of every stripe spend countless hours arguing about such issues when, I want to suggest, should be used to address larger cultural changes related to urban complexity. Glenn Smith, a leading missiologist living and working in Montréal, succinctly states, "As urban areas grew and their cultures extended their influence, Protestants and Roman Catholic churches were perceived as incapable of helping their congregants face the changes." (Smith, 2011, 270). Smith's insights reveal the need for new approaches for a city brimming with diversity which can easily fuel a type of fear often found in many churches.

The Urban Sprawl & Kingdom Expansion

As the reign of Jesus continues to take shape in our cities we are wise to pay attention to new expressions of Christian leadership needed for our changing urban spaces. Approximately one year ago my wife and I returned to *La Belle Province* with the deep burden to see a new church take root. With a personal knowledge of the unique ways religion has shaped the city, our prayers were focused on where we should be and what a new church in this growing urban landscape might look like. Eventually we decided to make our home in the fastest growing area north of Montréal called Laval.[41] What we did not anticipate was Laval's growing urban trajectory and its significant attraction for immigrants.[42] Now numbering just over 400,000 people, Laval is on a trajectory to become the second largest city in Quebec providing a rich reminder of the sprawling urbanization emerging in larger cities. This budding urban center is a hot spot for families, who continue to see Laval as an area to find affordable housing within the greater Montréal region.

At present the population of Montréal and surrounding region is nearing four million. Conversation regarding gentrification, with a focus on sustainable approaches of transportation, give rise to new emerging infrastructures. These larger conversations occurring in many of Canada's urban centers, should remind us that new modes for sustainable growth have always generated the need for creative reengagement with the message of Jesus and surrounding culture. Historians have noted how roads paved by Romans, the leading transportation innovation of the time, made it possible for the earliest gospel stories to spread. As one New Testament historian has noted, Paul

---

[41] Laval was originally named *Île Jésus*, the island of Jesus. Laval is Quebec's third largest city.
[42] 50% of Laval newborns have at least one parent with an immigrant background. See http://www.centraide-mtl.org/en/documents/4481/upload/documents/Profile-Laval-2014_14.pdf/.

"took advantage of the *Pax Romana*, the network of Roman roads and Roman colonies, to spread the gospel." (Witherington, 1998, 637). It is now apparent that the church is in need of new carriers for the gospel, beyond our present paradigms. But fresh engagement is only possible when we stop lamenting how things have changed and ask *why* they have changed and *how* we may have contributed to the changes.

As in the ancient Roman Empire, Christian communities have had to navigate dramatic change while being confronted with increased diversity. The Septuagint and the earliest documents of the church highlight key facets about how cultural change impacted linguistic realities and the larger Hebrew identity. These lessons offer hope for our own linguistic and cultural challenges. Montréal, the largest French-speaking city in North America, continues to attract new ethnic diversity which always brings to the surface questions about religious and linguistic preservation. Moreover, the pluralistic ideals enmeshed in linguistic difference fuel the debates concerning secular values, which provides practitioners and leaders with formidable challenges and opportunities. May the lesson of Pentecost ring true again: that God will use his Church to make himself known to the nations in the beauty of their diverse languages.

While every city has a unique 'flavor', some provide a glimpse of the future. Having pastored in diverse parts of Canada, Montréal and the surrounding region provide a unique test-bed for how the gospel might be rearticulated and reframed for future generations. In what follows I hope to provide three practical suggestions that flow from my present experience as a church planter in this city, seeking God's wisdom for leading in a changing culture.

Emerging Currents Requiring Theological Reflection

It seems arrogant to propose that any one person could capture the beautiful and complex dynamics that shape our cities, yet this work reminds us that we are wise to explore emerging trends. Our first challenge is that culture is always in motion and so are we. Given this movement, it can seem impossible to put one's finger on the issues that are shaping the city and its surroundings. Nonetheless, I will explore three currents that are critical if the church desires to regain a level of influence in this post-Christian context. 'Current', seems like an appropriate word to address the fluid and turbulent dynamics at work in Montréal. Oceanographers who study currents use devices that help measure the current strength and speed, noting that currents don't have to be fast to impact other patterns of oceanic movement. It's no different for the forces that are shaping our city.

The first current shaping Montréal's post-Christian ethos requires rethinking the essence of 'proclamation' in relation to the craft of preaching. Madonna's popular 80's song *Papa Don't Preach* seems to be the anthem of a generation who view 'preaching' as a negative way of forcing people to do things they don't want to do. Secondly, it is becoming clear that our present models of leadership and our approach to training future leaders are inadequate. This current is felt most intensively in the dwindling enrollment in Canadian theological schools and the lack of clarity around spiritual maturity, organization clarity, and fluid models of learning that are essential in this new world. Lastly, the current which weaves together multiculturalism and pluralism remains central for urban centers battling interreligious tensions. While the historical tensions between Protestants and Roman Catholics remain, Montréal provides an increasingly vibrant context for how new collaborative models that foster community engagement must focus on

Christ-centered unity. On expounding on each of these three currents, my prayer is that these observations will resonate and fuel something fresh for your own context.

Preaching in an Anti-Proclamation Age

In Québec, as in other parts of North America, we now live in an anti-proclamation world. Whether we like it or not, proclaiming something is so easily associated with protest. In that sense, proclamation is associated with being loud, aggressive, and at worst, dangerous.[43] Images of proclamation include yelling "from the roof top" or pulpit. Those adamant about proclaiming the good news can miss the undertones of this shift. Also, they fail to consider *how* the message of Jesus will be heard and *how* it may be interpreted in a context where proclamation has been coupled with oppressive and dictatorial styles and forces.

In our home with three boys I see this at work as one of my sons tries to "out proclaim" the other. What happens next? All communication breaks down! As every parent knows, it's a sign of maturity to stop, listen, and reflect before speaking or stating one's own perspective. For too long proclamation has meant we get to privilege our story over the stories – or voices – of others. Just because the winners get the microphone does not mean you will stick around and listen. And many have not stuck around, but they continue to listen to voices they feel are honest and reflective of their own experiences. It is often assumed that people who leave our churches don't want to hear the truth, or they just love to be entertained, but maybe they want to be part of the larger context that shapes learning, teaching, and preaching. A digital generation raised with access to knowledge at their finger tips no longer embrace a model

---

[43] Concerns about how proclaims one's religion can shape a dangerous ideology. http://www.cbc.ca/news/canada/montreal/islamic-extremism-delays-permit-for-montreal-muslim-centre-1.2936944.

of preaching as a lecture from a Moses like figure who came from a mountain.

As a teacher, pastor, and in the most general sense, a communicator, I am learning that while proclaiming the good news of Jesus is needful, it remains a risky method in the context of consumer marketing and our constant exposure to sales media. What we hope will be heard as good news so easily becomes skewed and misunderstood through the lenses of suspicion. For this reason preaching, when seen only as a form of proclamation, requires rethinking as we tackle the dynamics of communicating in our urban centers. Although I affirm that preaching the good news of Jesus is essential, to ignore this shifting current would lack pastoral responsibility. I want to suggest that one of the ways 'proclamation' can and must be restored as central will require allowing new and different voices to shape how we understand the text being proclaimed. The plurality of voices, especially those marginalized, helps give new credence to the power of the gospel to transcend any one particular outlook and to speak to all who will listen. (Ekblad, 2005, 51). We are wise to return to the words of Jesus when *he preached* and stated, "Repent of your sins and turn to God, for the Kingdom of Heaven is near." (Matthew 4:17, NLT). This invitation to turn from our own ways came with the unexpected reminder that God, in this inauguration of the Kingdom, was near. The nearing presence of God in Christ is so often hijacked by loud and domineering voices which emphasize repentance before a holy God without the remind of his desire to be near to us, his creation. Simply put, if God is near, proclamation can be done quietly with equal efficacy and perhaps *more* efficacy given the emerging context.

The Shifting Realities of Pastoral Leadership

A second current that must be considered as part of discerning the soul of this city relates to leadership. Unfortunately Montréal and the

Greater Montréal area have seen numerous public servants fall to corruption allegations and unethical behavior.[44] These public events are symbolic in ways that shape how people view leaders in other spheres of society. While the literature about leadership principals and leadership character abound, theological reflection for 21st century pastoral leadership lacks a richer conversation around systemic issues in the pressure cooker of urban realities.

The days of strong clerical influence are long gone in Québec. Smith observes, "In the years leading up to the Quiet Revolution, the number of priests rose from 4,000 in 1930 to 5,000 in 1945 to 8,400 in 1960. Today, there are less than 3,000 and the average age is 63 years." (Smith, 1997, 12). These trends are not reserved for Roman Catholics alone, Protestant leaders have had to wrestle with their own leadership challenges. At present, I am aware of three Protestant churches in Montréal that are juggling a leadership crisis which will have complex ramifications.

Research exploring the shifts in Protestant churches in Québec from 1980-1997 reveal, a growing need for well-trained leadership for ministry in urban contexts. (Smith, 1998, 245). Baptist Missions documents from the 1960s revealed the lack of planning and financial resources for training leaders in Montréal's unique context. (Randall & Cross, 2008, 198). The strategic and personal challenges remain, and only when we have open and sustained dialogue will we find our way out of these old 'wineskins' to new leadership paradigms. In changing times, the gift of pastoral leadership becomes more attuned to the way the Holy Spirit's is at work in the life of the people both in the church and those outside the traditional church settings. Wheatley, who has done

---

[44] Laval's former mayor awaits trial. http://www.cbc.ca/news/canada/montreal/city-of-laval-lawsuit-gilles-vaillancourt-1.3288690.

extensive work on change managements remarks, "A good leader supports a continuous conversation about organizational identity and how it is changing as it does its work in a changing world." (Wheatley, 2005, 83).

The old training methods often associated with denominational schools of thought are no longer adequate or sustainable Christ centered impact in urban centers. The philosophical and hermeneutical battles around the perspicuity of scripture creates entrenched political camps leading to blame games that paralyze us. Meanwhile we fail to engage intelligently with the tidal wave of change, which is something the scriptures address. As social media giant Facebook reveals fifty gender types to choose from, many continue to adhere to stereotypes, or hide behind the so-called banner of truth. This is not the time to deny biblical authority, but it is time to listen anew to one another and to seek how the empowerment of the Spirit will empower as we seek to develop wise leaders who can weave new stories of hope with a focus on the urgent issues of our day.

Pastoral leaders who will shape kingdom minded disciples must learn to emphasize the ways of thinking that have either helped or misdirected our engagement with our cities. This type of leadership which is both Christ-centered and community conscious will require new levels of courage so that Jesus' love can be understood and embraced. Québec has "one of the lowest birthrates in the world and ... one of the highest rates of abortion among the industrialized countries." (Tentler, 2007, 6). How we address and care for this deep kind of wound requires an understanding of what got us here in the first place. In that sense, the next generation of pastoral leadership will require a keen sense of self-awareness and honesty. In so doing, I believe, a return to a theology of pastoral discernment will remain critical for leaders addressing the soul of this city. However, we can't underestimate how difficult it will be to rearticulate and re-contextualize the story of Jesus within a culture committed to secular values.

A Collaborative Christ-Centeredness

The third current relates to grappling with the growing inter-religious context and our need for a thoughtful approach that can 'comfortably' cross boundaries and encourage dialogue and understanding. In 2007 a booklet entitled *Le dialogue interreligieux dans un Québec pluraliste* (*An interreligious dialogue about a pluralistic Québec*) attempted to address the new multi-religious realities of urban life in the province. The Roman Catholic Bishops of Québec who wrote this document remind us how interreligious difference must be squarely faced if we want to see our cities flourish. One revelation was that between 1980 and 2001 the number of those who consider themselves Muslims has doubled.[45] The landscape that has emerged in this urban center requires a collaborative attitude among new religious communities. I believe that this is a prerequisite for God honoring leadership, committed to dialogue and peace-making in urban centers in Canada.

For the churches that have failed to embrace conversation partners from *within* the diversity of Christianity this new urban reality will likely feel daunting. McAlpine, a fellow contributor to this collection, notes "an apparent increased openness to ecumenical dialogue and an openness to, and even longing for, spiritual experience that transcends denominational or traditional boundaries " is already at work. (McAlpine, 2011, 134). This hunger for spiritual experience and for dialogue does not mean that we ignore or wash away difference. Rather

---

[45]From the Assembly of the Roman Catholic Bishops of Québec. Le dialogue interreligieux dans un Québec pluralists. (Montreal: Mediapaul, 2007, 9). "... une forte croissance des populations musulmanes—plus du double."

it is our love for Jesus and his command to love each other that helps us celebrate and critique the realities of the post-secular marketplace when our difference may lead to division. Learning to live in the tension of diversity has helped me to gain a prophetic viewpoint that informs difficult discussions. In this light, secularization may provide the nudge we need to imagine something beyond our present structures and rigid boundaries.

Philosopher Charles Taylor, a Montréaler himself, provides further insight into the challenges related to faith and our changing urban centers. For Taylor the three currents mentioned above will be confronted with multicultural realities which will stretch us to be ""transformed by the study of the other, so that we are not simply judging by our original familiar standards." (Taylor, 1994, 71). This is again consistent with Jesus invitation to love our neighbor. Only when we practice a kind of love that creates new spaces of learning *not* filled with pre-conceived prejudice can a commitment to a new collaborative approach that is Christ-centered take shape. If we empty ourselves we will have space for both Jesus and our neighbor.

For a city often associated with a model of secularization, it can come as a surprise that a collective religious memory is still strongly at work in this province. As the city prepared for Montréal's 375th anniversary in 2017, a proposal suggested the need to renovate St. Joseph's Oratory, one of Canada's largest church buildings at the heart of city of Montréal. The estimated cost of 80 million dollars[46] would preserve this religious space: symbolic of our age trying to find its place in their unique religious heritage. While many remain perplexed as to

---

46 Federal government will donate $22 million, Québec is investing $30.8 million and Montréal will contribute $10 million to the oratory's Great Development Project. St. Joseph's Oratory will contribute $26.4 million. See http://Montréalgazette.com/news/local-news/st-josephs-oratory-to-get-millions-for-Montréals-375th-anniversary.

why a city committed to a secular future would entertain such a conversation, yet here lay the complex and unique nature of a city like Montréal. One in which a desire to hold on to something transcendent remind us that our fragmented order gives the Church and her leaders the rare opportunity to offer a meaningful alternative way to live in the power of covenant communities centered on a God who meets us where we are.

References

Baum, Gregory. (2014). *Truth and Relevance: Catholic Theology in French Quebec Since the Quiet Revolution.* Montreal: McGill – Queens University Press.

Cox. Harvey. (2009). *The Future of Faith.* New York: Harper Collins Publishing.

Ekblad, Bob Jr. (2005). *Reading the Bible with the Damned.* Louisville, KY: Westminster: John Knox Press.

Newbigin, Lesslie. (1961). *Is Christ Divided?: A Plea for Christian Unity in a Revolutionary Age.* Grand Rapids: Eerdmans Publishing.

Lougheed, Richard. (2011). Clashes in Worldview: French Protestants and Roman Catholics in the 19th Century. *French- Speaking Protestants in Canada: Historical Essays.* Jason Zuidema, Ed. Boston MA: Brill.

McAlpine, William R. (2011). *Sacred Space for the Missional Church: Engaging Culture through the Building Environment.* Eugene, OR: Wipf & Stock Publishers.

Randall, Ian M and Anthony R. Cross, Eds. (2008). Papers from the Fourth International Conference on Baptist Studies. *Studies in Baptist History and Thought.* Vol. 29. Eugene, OR: Wipf & Stock Publishers.

Sancton, Andrew. (1984). *Governing the Island of Montreal: Language Differences and Metropolitan Politics.* Berkeley: Institute of International Studies.

Schmitt, Eric-Emmanuel. (September 2014). *L'Heureux Naufrage.* http://www.heureuxnaufrage.com/en

Smith, Glenn. (2011). A Brief Socio-Demographic Portrait of French Speaking Protestantism in Quebec since 1960. *French- Speaking Protestants in Canada: Historical Essays.* Jason Zuidema, Ed. Boston, MA: Brill.

Smith, Glenn. (1998). The Québec Protestant Church. *Transforming Our Nation: Empowering the Canadian Church for a Greater Harvest.* Murray Moerman, Ed. Richmond, BC.

Smith, Glenn. (Summer 1997). *How Unique is Québec's Religious Climate Anyway?* Montreal: Christian Direction.

Smith, James K. (2006). *You Are What You Love: The Spiritual Power of Habit*. Grand Rapids, MI: Brazos Press.

Taylor, Charles. (1994). The Politics of Recognition'. *Multiculturalism: Examining the Politics of Recognition*, ed. Amy Gutmann, Princeton, NJ: Princeton University Press.

Tentler, Leslie W. (2007). *The Church Confronts Modernity*. Washington, DC: The Catholic University of America Press.

Witherington, Ben. (1998). *The Acts of the Apostles*. Grand Rapids, MI: Eerdmans Publishing.

Wheatley, Margaret J. (2005). *Finding our Way: Leadership for an Uncertain Time*. San Francisco, CA: Berrett-Koehler Publishing.

CHAPTER ELEVEN

Halifax, Nova Scotia

Gary Thorne

Halifax, the capital city of Nova Scotia, is a city of nearly half a million people who live in many diverse, small communities within the municipality. Halifax has a soul that underlies and shapes this diversity, embodied in an identifiable contemplative spirit that runs out into a generous, compassionate way of living.

If you are visiting Halifax by train, or even arriving on one of the many cruise ships, the first site you might visit, just across from the station and up from the harbour, is a statue of Edward Cornwallis, who founded Halifax in 1749. This rather unremarkable sculpture is found in many small towns in North America. A bronze representation of an aristocratic 18th-century army officer, it stands twenty feet tall on its pedestal, gazing confidently across a park. Today this nondescript symbol is deeply contested, and often stained by paint or graffiti. Cornwallis had issued a bounty on the scalps of all Mi'kmaq First Nations people – men, women, and children. Halifax thus participates in the legacy of genocide, a nation coming to terms with its own genocidal past.

Cornwallis is a contradictory figure, representing both the foresight and courage of the settlers, and colonial violence. Keep the statue or pull it down? The universities now regularly announce that they are on the unceded territory of the Mi'qmaq people; many official events are now incomplete without drumming and a chant from a First Nations representative. Schools and streets once named after

Cornwallis are now having his name removed. His legacy in the city provokes continuous debate. Nevertheless, that Edward Cornwallis continues to stand in the park despite the controversy tells us of another aspect of the soul of Halifax as a contested space: under pressure to conform to the universalizing values of globalization while adhering to its unique character. Let us explore the city before attempting to describe her soul more fully.

Just blocks away from this statue is another symbolic location, right on the edge of the harbour. Pier 21 is one of only three national museums outside the nation's capital. A million people seeking to establish a new homeland in Canada arrived at this pier from 1928 to 1971. The museum presents remarkable stories of these immigrants. Many passed through Halifax, but some stayed, and the city's social mix grew out of this influx. Today, Canadians are looking to immigration as one of the solutions to our struggling economy. Yet are immigrants welcome? In some parts of Halifax they are eagerly supported; in others viewed with suspicion. Unlike many other Canadian cities, Halifax is still caught in between. This ambivalence does not rise from a thoughtless conservatism, but from a contemplative spirit that refuses to be hurried. Pier 21 looks at the way our ancestors were welcomed, and also at the difficulties they faced upon arrival. In Halifax, the practice of deep compassion requires an equally deep practice of unhurried contemplation.

If you were to take a taxi northward from Pier 21 for about 2 kilometres, along a rambling road that parallels the shoreline to the base of one of our two bridges, you would arrive at a small park. This is the remnant of Africville, a settlement that former American slaves established just outside Halifax after the War of 1812. By the mid 1960s, the impoverished conditions of Africville were a source of deep shame for the city. Its residents had no running water, no sewage system, no garbage pickup, no streetlights, no public transportation and no paved roads. Instead, there was an open dump, an incinerator, a prison, railway tracks, and an abattoir. Instead of making improvements, Halifax city officials decided to raze Africville. By 1967, after several years of study and talk, the 400 citizens of Africville were relocated, their houses and all community buildings were demolished, and the residents were forced into public housing. All that is left now is an official monument and a tidy church, rebuilt as a replica of the Baptist Church that was the center of this once spirited, intimate, and eccentric community.

The tragedy of Africville's unjust destruction is recognized by locals as a failure of the contemplative spirit, and it continues to define race relations in Halifax today. Unlike many other parts of Canada, Nova Scotia has had a significant, proud, established black community stretching back to the eighteenth century, but it is still in the process of defining itself in relation to the largely white and privileged majority. Throughout North America, black communities gained great rights and recognition in the 1960s and 1970s through civic unrest and courageous affirmative action. Admission of overt and covert racism has only gradually been recognized by the political powers. This is true in Halifax also. Change has come slowly, but the contemplative spirit of Halifax has been enriched by a profound repentance for the destruction of Africville and all that it represents.

Just a few steps away from the Africville Park is another place barely acknowledged by townsmen or tourists. This is ground zero of the Halifax Explosion of 1917, the greatest man-made combustion before the arrival of the atomic bomb. Two ships collided in the harbor; one was carrying a massive cargo of bomb-making materials. Thousands of people were killed across the city, and large areas near the harbour were completely flattened. The response was extraordinary, with aid arriving from many Canadian and American cities (particularly Boston, to which Nova Scotia annually gives a massive Christmas Tree as a thanksgiving). The site is now a park, a quiet spot in the city, conducive to meditation. It is marked by a small monument of bells at the top of the hill. Many of the reminders of the explosion have been obliterated, and Ground Zero is now the location of a massive facility (ironically) for the construction of warships.

From its start as an English city, Halifax has served as a protected harbour for international shipping. This industry is nothing like it was in the past, but the town still has two facilities for containers, and the naval yards remain active (they run along much of the road between the Cornwallis statue and the site of Africville). But the role of the city has changed. It is the leading provincial capital of the Maritime Provinces, and government and branches of national and international organizations are the principal economic drivers. These are not normally the places one looks for "soul." There are also schools, a surprising number of universities, a lively arts community, and churches throughout the city. The religious life of the place has always been important, whether it concerns the indigenous Mi'qmaq communities, the early visitors from France and England, or the waves of nineteenth-century immigrants. These historical events help us to understand the underlying nature of recurring themes in the city's life. But more recent developments have been especially interesting for anyone seeking the signs of the spiritual: the arrival of Shambhala Buddhists in the eighties, and the recent increase in the number of university students who remain in Halifax after completing their studies. Both groups evince their own unique ethos, a commitment to social justice aligned with a peculiar secular life and lifestyle.

The Soul of the City

Trungpa Rinpoche is credited with introducing Tibetan Buddhism to the Western world. He was recognized in his native Tibet as the Eleventh Trunga Tulka, an enlightened being who has voluntarily returned to human form to teach others the path out of suffering. He trained extensively in the three major schools of Buddhism – hinayana, mahayana, and vajayana – and was forced into exile by the Chinese Communists in 1959 (along with the Dalai Lama). He eventually moved to America in 1970 where, traveling almost constantly from his chosen base in Boulder, Colorado, he was to become the most significant teacher of Tibetan Buddhism in North America. Trungpa offered the essence of the highest Buddhist teachings in a form readily understandable to Western students: meditation and philosophy stripped of its religious trappings. My colleague David Swick (1996) speaks of the extraordinary flowering of this teaching in affluent America:

> The early 1970s were a time of spiritual shopping among young people, and everywhere Trungpa spoke he found people eager to become his students. Most were unkempt, hairy, fond of recreational drugs, and profoundly hungry to learn. The keenest of these inevitably moved to Boulder [Colorado] to take a summer course or to live near more Buddhists. By 1979 the city of 75,000 had a Buddhist community of more than 1,500. Not counting children and the university population, one in every twenty-five Boulderites was a Buddhist. Trungpa's students loved it. Boulder offered spectacular scenery, spiritual teaching, and material luxury to boot. What could be better than that? (p. 14)

Evidently, at least in the eyes of their spiritual leader, a small and seemingly conservative city called Halifax, Nova Scotia.

After years of visiting cities throughout North America and Australia, the spiritual head of international Shambala Buddhism chose Halifax as the place most suited to the practice of Bhuddhist meditation and contemplation. Thus it became the headquarters of the worldwide Tibetan Buddhist organization, Vajradhatu International (since renamed Shambhala International). By the mid-eighties, hundreds had followed Trungpa to Halifax, forming the largest resident non-Asian Buddhist community in the world. But what was it about the soul of Halifax that convinced Trungpa it was ripe for, and already on the way to, enlightenment?

This question is still being asked by the Buddhist immigrants 30 years later. A prevalent speculation is that Trungpa found Boulder too young, fit, hip, white, complacent, comfortable, and affluent to become the enlightened community his teaching promised to establish. Halifax was more rugged, had a slower pace of life, was less steeped in the powerful consumerism of the US, and reflected a compassionate gentleness more consistent with the principles of the teaching and practices of Shambhala Buddhism. Perhaps Trunpga also recognized that the winter climate of ice and snow inculcated an almost Nordic sense of meditative thoughtfulness.

Clearly, in Halifax Trungpa saw the possibility of creating an "enlightened society" free of competitiveness, greed, aggression and arrogance. The testimonies of the Boulderites who followed their spiritual Master to Halifax consistently reflect the adjustment that they and their families gradually made to the simpler, natural, gentle, relational, and non-materialistic Haligonian lifestyle. If this more sustainable and balanced existence is what prompted Trungpa to relocate to Halifax, then there is no doubt that the significant presence of the Buddhist community in the last few decades has deepened and strengthened the city's contemplative spirit and compassionate way of life.

This contemplative compassion, manifest in a creative and artistic civic spirit, attracts many to Halifax, and surely explains why an unusually high number of young university graduates settle here after graduating from one of the city's six universities. During their university years, the place captures and shapes their imaginations with a vision of the Good and the Beautiful that resonates with a refreshing 'New Secularism'[47], a perspective that seeks to re-enchant both Nature and City with a sense of wonder, hope and excitement. These young graduates contribute to a spiritual (perhaps even "mystical") meaning to the mechanistic material sterility of the secularity of much of the twentieth century. Their experience of an undeniable, though indefinable, reality of 'transcendence' determines their uncompromising commitment to honoring and caring for the natural order, for the city, and for one another.

Increasingly for students in the early 21st century, the notion of vocation is tied to the discovery of meaningful place and commitment to the values of the community in which a person will live, and no longer defined by the job or career that a person seeks. Clearly, students do not choose to remain in Halifax for economic reasons. In the ten years since 2006 all of the net employment growth in the city has been absorbed by those over the age of 45.

Underemployment is so rampant that baristas are unionizing. These young people from across Canada and the United States remain in Halifax because they experience the city as a place of nourishment, healing, and compassionate community. They significantly define and shape the soul of Halifax in creative, artistic ways, akin to the contribution of the Buddhist immigrants described above.

It has been suggested that Trungpa Rinpoche choose Halifax because he "did a careful measuring of the earth's energy lines, and realized Nova Scotia lies in the crosshairs of an overflow of positive

---

[47] 'New Secularism' is not a movement but a term I coined to highlight what I perceive in most non-religious university students as a robust secularism that is open to the wonder of an undefined yet powerful immanence and transcendence in the natural order and human community, as opposed to the secularism of the previous generation that was a rather sterile secularity committed to the 'absence' of God and unwilling to consider any notion of immanence or transcendence.

energy." (Swick, 1996, p. 19) As bizarre as that might seem, many students are similarly hard-pressed to articulate their experience of transcendence and immanence in Halifax, forces that powerfully holds them here. Ernest Buckler was one of Canada's best-known twentieth-century novelists, mostly famous for *The Mountain and the Valley*. In an interview with Donald Cameron, he made the strange claim that "in the Nova Scotia country … you get the universals more than you do almost anywhere else." (Cameron, 1973, p. 8) "Universals" or Platonic ideal forms are another way of speaking of immanence and transcendence, and this seems an attraction for the young.

As has happened across Western culture, there has been an extraordinary loosening up of social discourse which offers freedom, including the freedom to search. But sometimes the search for novel sexual experience or other things can displace or stand in for other kinds of searching. A rich secular culture leads in many directions.

The city shows this mix. The music scene in Halifax is ambitious and multifarious. Halifax is the largest arts and culture venue east of Montreal. Northend Halifax is one of the few truly integrated interracial communities in Canada. Run-down older inner-city neighbourhoods of twenty years ago are becoming gentrified and marketed as Halifax's "chic arts districts" as higher income people are attracted by the 'artsy, quirky and diverse.' Haligonians happily and fully comply with the city's robust composting, limited garbage, and recycling policy. There is cultural vibrancy, a cool nightlife, great restaurants, plenty of farm markets, fresh fish markets, full-service butcher shops offering local sustainably raised meats, and many bike shops. There is also both the oldest lighthouse and the oldest Martello Tower in North America. On the one hand Halifax is rooted in a rich history and is zealous of a traditional way of life; on the other hand it is substantially a naval and a university town that is accustomed to welcoming strangers and embracing cultural and ethnic diversity.

This increasingly welcoming city also has opened up to other religions. The deepening cultural variety of the city is signaled by two of the most stunningly beautiful new buildings in Halifax: a Mosque and an Antiochian Orthodox Church. The two are situated less than a block apart, and just fifty metres away from a traditional Buddhist Temple (not Shambhala). The large Antiochian Orthodox Church, bursting at its seams with worshippers, is on the site of an abandoned Anglican Church, and the Buddhist Temple is a converted Presbyterian Church building.

I have tried to indicate, however briefly, how the spiritual complexity of present-day Halifax has evolved. But is there a 'soul' to Halifax, and if so, what is the vision of the ideal City by which we judge the soul of a particular one? By what standards can we judge the extent to which a city has a contemplative spirit or compassionate character? How do we judge if it needs a deepening conversion, i.e. a greater turning toward the Good, the Beautiful and the True? What is the Good, the Beautiful and the True for a city?

In the 1970s, my Haligonian colleagues at the University of King's College, where I have been Chaplain since 2005, introduced me to the image of the city as described by Charles Williams in his poetry, novels, and theological writings (Williams, 1958). For Williams, the soul of a city is defined in terms of the three related principles of co-inherence (mutual-indwelling), exchange, and substitution. In the remainder of this chapter I shall describe these meanings and attempt to situate the soul of Halifax within Williams' theology.

"Co-inherence" is the mutual indwelling of all persons in one another, including all the interaction and interdependence with one another. As the Blessed Persons of the Holy Trinity co-inhere in one another, and as the divine and human natures of Christ co-inhere in one another, so humans co-inhere in one another. This is an ontological fact – the natural human condition - and not a choice to be made. Williams was fond of quoting St Anthony, "Your life and your death are with your neighbour" (Williams, 1958, p. 109).

"Exchange" is the voluntary giving and taking by which we express our co-inherent citizenship in the city; its modes include substitution, sacrifice, forgiveness, and reconciliation. The choice that a citizen makes is either to affirm the truth of co-inherence in acts of love, or to reject its truth in failure to act lovingly.

"Substitution" is the mode of exchange that involves a literal interpretation of the New Testament command to "Bear one another's burdens" (Gal 6:2). The doctrine of co-inherence insists that we can take on another's burdens of pain, anxiety, grief, and fear. Just as in the physical sphere we can carry a heavy parcel for another, fully bearing the whole weight relieving the other of its weight entirely, so "substitution" is the carrying of another's emotional and spiritual burdens of pain, anxiety, grief, and fear.

Thus the soul of any city is defined by the doctrine of co-inherence. The city is the place where people make compacts to bear one another's burdens. An important aspect of both exchange and substitution is that citizens must learn how to live *from* others, as much as how to live *for* others. "Both are necessary to the perfect exchange. The methods of exchange, of carrying burdens and of giving up burdens to be carried..." (Williams, 1958, p. 107). Thus, the specific character of soul of any particular city is determined by the fullness of the city's openness to, and the particular expressions of, exchange or substitution by which the doctrine of co-inherence is acknowledged and strengthened through acts of love, or denied and weakened through a failure to act lovingly. The life of the city is precisely the life of co-inherence: there is no escaping, but only either a deepening or weakening of that life.

The Soul of the City

Thus Christ weeps over the holy City of Jerusalem in Luke 19, and he weeps over Halifax today insomuch as its citizens do not acknowledge the truth of their co-inherence (mutual in-dwelling in one another) in their daily practice of exchange and substitution in the city. The ideal or redeemed City is that of perfect exchange and substitution. Williams refers to the redeemed city of the heavenly Jerusalem of Revelation 21, "The principle of that City ... is the doctrine that no man lives to himself or indeed *from* himself. This is the doctrine common to nature and grace." (Williams, 1958, p. 104).

So how does the soul of Halifax fare according to Williams' theology? In the remainder of this chapter I shall share my own experience of Halifax in terms of Williams' doctrine of co-inherence, specifically as Rector of Saint George's Round Church in Halifax' inner city.

In the telling of my story it is important to note that throughout my 35 years of ministry I have understood that the principles of exchange and substitution that contribute to the vision of the redeemed City are the same principles that contribute to the spiritual health of the Body of Christ in a particular parish. It is all about relationship and the integrity of the created order. "Bearing one another's burdens" is the fulfillment both of the law of the City, and of the law of Christ (Gal 4:1). It is true that members of the parish are constantly reminded of the life of co-inherence in the sacraments of Baptism and Eucharist where Divine Exchange and Substitution are made visible and effectual, yet it is so important to note that for Williams co-inherence is the *universal vision* of the natural city. It simply *is* the soul of the city, whether recognized or not, and is able to be recognized not only by Christians but by all citizens equally, regardless of their particular faith or deeply held convictions. I begin my story with a brief glance at the history of Saint

George's parish in the 20th century. This story also offers a glimpse into how the city more broadly has changed over the years.

Called the Round Church because of its remarkable architectural form, the first half of the 20th century was a busy time at Saint George's, with large congregations and Sunday Schools, established choirs, and extensive ministries. During the following half century, the situation changed dramatically. The city's new-found commitment to a narrow program of urban renewal meant not only the destruction of Africville, but also the demolition of many working-class residential areas. Demographic shifts to the suburbs gained momentum from 1950-1980, and Saint George's found itself no longer "downtown," but in an economically depressed "inner city" or "urban core." Even with the construction of several large high-rises for seniors, and the influx of African Nova Scotians into public housing in nearby Uniacke Square and Mulgrave Park (due to their forced re-location from Africville), the population of the North End fell by 42% between 1961 and 1976. Enrollment at North End schools dropped by as much as 75%, and several closed. Social stigma attached to public housing and the increasing crime caused every bank branch and supermarket to close. Telephone booths were removed from the area because of repeated vandalism.

Saint George's white, established, middle-class neighbourhood congregation had disappeared. The church barely survived. In the early 1980s, the congregation that travelled in from the suburbs on Sunday mornings was aging and increasingly isolated from the surrounding neighbourhood. All its buildings were old and dilapidated, and it was in significant debt. The closing of the parish seemed certain, until a former Halifax university chaplain was appointed Rector. Father Robert Petite was a young progressive priest whose university connections attracted students and faculty.

The Soul of the City

The university crowd consisted of avant-garde intellectuals shaped by the New Secularism of their generation, ready to explore spiritual transcendence in elaborate ritual and music. Saint George's was caught up in the same spiritual openness that was attracting the Shambhala Buddhists to the city. But Father Petite proved to be too progressive for some. When he boldly took the parish into the city (and brought the city into the parish) with his courageous chaplaincy to the community of HIV-infected and persons with AIDS, his compassionate actions elicited a rushed response that was inconsistent with the unhurried contemplative spirit of the parish and city. Thus most of the parishioners left, Father Petite resigned, and the parish again seemed destined for closure.

In 1989 I accepted the offer to become Rector of Saint George's Parish. It was an easy decision. I had become discouraged from two years as an assistant curate in a large urban church where I witnessed the brightest and best in the church hierarchy facilitating deep dysfunction. Alarming and destructive pathologies in the congregation were fueled in turn by the spiritual leadership. Co-inherence, exchange and substitution were neither preached nor practiced. I decided to look for employment outside this church.

The invitation to build a congregation from scratch was unexpected and irresistible. I intended to build on the principles of co-inherence, exchange and substitution at an historic church building in the heart of the most economically depressed inner city neighbourhood in Halifax. It was a difficult path I set down, but it brought me right to the heart of an evolving Halifax.

I shall share five brief vignettes that illustrate my seventeen years of attempting to realize a vision of the redeemed City in a Halifax parish church. The first two vignettes are cautionary tales.

Williams is clear about the inclusiveness of the City. In the first months I met individually with all members of the congregation who almost without exception told me that the parish would only survive if a certain individual was removed. She was presented to me as someone with an obsession to control, with compulsive lying, passive-aggressive behavior, and her manipulation was said to have brought the parish to the point of closure. The exchange and substitution of co-inherence was not her *modus operandi*! Nonetheless, during my initial interviews with the few remaining parishioners I had the opportunity to speak of my vision of the parish as radically inclusive: even inclusive of a person who might set out to destroy the parish itself.

About this time the leading North American 'institutes for church leadership and congregational growth' were encouraging congregations to rid themselves of such individuals who stood in the way of healthy spiritual development: they were likened to cancers that should be removed. All of the pathologies and vices proved to be present in this individual. For seventeen years she made life extraordinarily difficult for me and my family. Her attitude and behavior caused many parishioners to leave the parish, but she remained. As we intentionally reduced her ability to do harm through a judicious re-establishment of roles, she began to contribute to parish community in more healthy ways, though her pathologies were always present. Co-inherence was acknowledged and meaningful exchange was practiced. In the right context she manifested a willingness and ability to bear the burdens of others. The City is inclusive, even if such inclusivity is difficult to achieve.

The second vignette is that of a cold winter's evening on the second Sunday in Advent in my first year. I arrived to prepare for the choral Advent Procession with Carols. I was greeted by a warden who told me with considerable glee that he had successfully chased away the prostitutes from one of their favorite corners near the entrance of the Church, so that church-goers would not be discouraged from attending church. I rushed out to apologize and invite them back, but they had disappeared. In subsequent years the congregation would learn that the principles of co-inherence, exchange and substitution extended to all persons. The parish eventually became passionate advocates of sex-workers' rights, sat on the Board of its supporting organization, held an annual Christmas Party for the sex-workers along with their partners and children, and generally began to develop real friendships.

The third vignette is a tragic event, by which we were divinely blessed. On June 2, 1994 three boys aged 7, 8, and 9, all well known to the parish, set fire to the Church. This National Historic Site (the church had been designed by the father of Queen Victoria) was almost entirely destroyed. On the news we immediately offered pardon and forgiveness (and were condemned in the local media for being too soft). A nearby church was outraged when we announced we would rebuild: "Feed the poor with the insurance money" was the message from the neighbouring pulpit. Instead, at the weekly soup kitchen two days later, a street-person (and friend) to whom I had given countless change in the past, handed me a loonie: "Let this be the first loonie to rebuild our church," he said. And it was. Throughout the restoration of the Round Church the congregation practiced the principles of co-inherence, exchange, and substitution in countless ways and acts of love. We fought hard against the condescending assumption that persons in poverty, on the street, or in the working class cannot find deep meaning in poetry, liturgical language, or in rich choral music. Persons who find themselves in poverty are very capable of enjoying an imaginative life nourished by exposure to beauty, art, music, poetry and vision. Dr. Margaret Casey, the Director of the North End Health Clinic tried to teach us this in the simple note she sent the day after the fire. Casey, a champion for those who found themselves most vulnerable and dispossessed in our neighbourhood, encouraged us to do everything we could to restore the Round Church. She urged us on the grounds that roses are as necessary in our lives as bread. I saw her two and a half years later at a graveside. In our chatting, I started to list some of the things Saint George's was doing, probably thinking our activities would please her. In a kind but firm way, she reminded me that the very beauty of this church and the loveliness of our worship helps to create the possibility for co-inherence, exchange, and substitution.

The fourth vignette came about during the establishment of a youth program, when we had to resist constant pressure. Why not simply employ black youth workers? What would a predominately white, middle class, highly-educated congregation that worships with elaborate liturgy and sophisticated music have to offer to inner city youth? The answer was clear to us. We offered ourselves in friendship, in all our white middle-classness. The result has been wonderfully successful as parishioners and local youth have shared in countless adventures including wilderness hikes, extended back-country camping, day-programs, tutoring, musicals, art shows, and leadership training. Even Greek and Latin classes have been shared with junior high school students. The program followed the principles of co-inherence, exchange, and substitution.

The fifth and final vignette is the establishment of Halifax Humanities 101. This project was modelled on the Clemente course in humanities founded in New York by the late Earl Shorris. The program offers barrier-free university level instruction in the humanities to people who live on assistance, disability, pension, or have other financial restraints or mental health conditions, conditions that put the regular university classroom out of reach. The best professors from Halifax's six universities now lobby to teach these eager students. The students make

The Soul of the City

extraordinary sacrifices in time and effort to participate in this year-long study. The instructors are engaged by the sophistication of the insights brought to them by these marginalized students who live in material poverty. The acknowledgement of mutual co-inherence is realized and lived out in the mutuality of friendships, exchanges, and reciprocal carrying of burdens.

In Scripture and in the writings of Charles Williams, "The City" is here and now and eternal; it is a life in which its citizens express their unity in their lives and interactions. Williams said, "here citizenship meant relationship and knew it." The ways of the Holy City are sacrifice, forgiveness, and reconciliation. The City is both a way of order and hierarchy, and also what Williams expressed as "that joyous smile of equality which marks all happy human or celestial government" and "where everything and everyone is unique and is the subject of due adoration." (Williams, 1958).

In my time at Saint George's I discovered a people open to the practice of exchange and substitution by which they came increasingly to be convinced of co-inherence as the soul and life of the city of Halifax. Although most Haligonians might not articulate the reality of the soul of the city in such terms, I have indicated that spiritually-attuned persons of various traditions sense something very special about Halifax. I think this is best summed up as a contemplative spirit that leads to a radical compassion. This contemplation and compassion is what shapes our engagement with our past. It has led the city to a thorough repentance for its treatment of the black community. The Buddhists and the university students sense this contemplative spirit and compassionate soul, and I have learned to recognize it through my own action in the heart of the city.

One hundred years ago the Reverend Samuel Prince was an Anglican priest at King's College who founded the Maritime School of

Hjalmarson

Social Work. In his extensive doctoral thesis at the University of Columbia in New York on the aftermath of the Halifax Disaster of 1917, he came to know the soul of Halifax perhaps better than anyone before or since. In the dedication of his monograph to the citizens of Halifax we read the simple truth:

> *Halifax is not a large city*
> *but there are those who love it*
> *who would choose to dwell therein*
> *before all the cities beneath the skies*

References

Cameron, David. (1973). *Conversations with Canadian Novelists.* Toronto: MacMillan.

Swick, David. (1996). *Thunder and Ocean: Shambhala & Buddhism in Nova Scotia.* Halifax, NS: Lawrencetown Press.

Williams, Charles. (1958). *The Image of the City and other Essays.* London: Oxford University Press.

www.ingramcontent.com/pod-product-compliance
Lightning Source LLC
Chambersburg PA
CBHW070141100426
42743CB00013B/2790